D0226083

4-91

EGYPTIAN
MUMMIES

WITHDRAWN

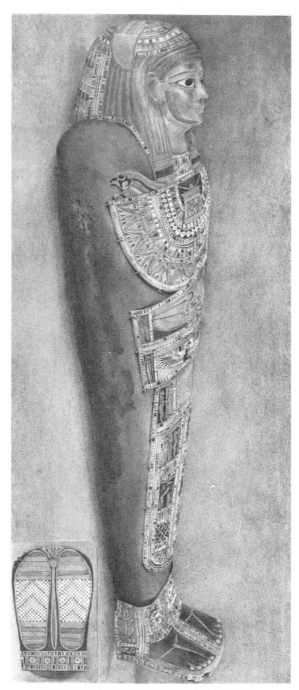

PTOLEMAIC MUMMY IN CARTONNAGE CASING

EGYPTIAN MUMMIES

G. Elliot Smith

and

Warren R. Dawson

Kegan Paul International
London and New York

WOODBRIDGE TOWN LIBRARY
10 NEWTON ROAD
WOODBRIDGE, CT 06525

First published in 1924
This edition published in 1991 by
Kegan Paul International Ltd
PO Box 256, London WC1B 3SW, England

Distributed by
John Wiley & Sons Ltd
Southern Cross Trading Estate
1 Oldlands Way, Bognor Regis,
West Sussex, PO22 9SA, England

Routledge, Chapman & Hall Inc
29 West 35th Street
New York, NY 10001, USA

The Canterbury Press Pty Ltd
Unit 2, 71 Rushdale Street
Scoresby, Victoria 3179, Australia

This edition Kegan Paul International 1991

Printed in Great Britain by TJ Press (Padstow) Ltd, Padstow,
Cornwall.

No part of this book may be reproduced in any form without
permission from the publisher, except for the quotation of
brief passages in criticism.

British Library Cataloguing in Publication Data
Smith, G. Elliott
Egyptian mummies.
1.Egyptian mummies, ancient period
I. Title II. Dawson, Warren R. (Warren Royal)
393.30932
ISBN 0-7103-0410-2
US Library of Congress Cataloging in Publication Data
Applied for

"*A* GREAT *part of antiquity contented their hopes of subsistency with a transmigration of their souls, a good way to continue their memories.*

"*Egyptian ingenuity was more unsatisfied, continuing their bodies in sweet consistencies to attend the return of their souls.*

"*But all was vanity, feeding the wind, and folly.*

"*The Egyptian mummies, which Cambyses or time hath spared, avarice now consumeth.*

"*Mummy is become merchandise, Mizraim cures wounds, and Pharaoh is sold for Balsams.*"—(Sir Thomas Browne, 1658.)

In his book with the formidable title "*NEKPOKHΔEIA;* or, the Art of Embalming; wherein is shewn the Right of Burial, the Funeral Ceremonies and the several ways of Preserving Dead Bodies in most Nations of the World, with an Account of the particular Opinions, Experiments and Inventions of Modern Physicians, Surgeons, Chymists and Anatomists, also some new Matter proposed concerning a better method of Embalming than hath hitherto been discovered, and a Pharmacopoeia Galeno-Chymica Anatomia sicca sive incruenta, etc.," Thomas Greenhill in 1705 discussed the possible ways in which embalming may have originated :—

"(1) Necessity, *the mother of Invention may have driven men to render their dead innocuous to themselves ;*

"(2) Unexpected Results of Experiments, *as when you aim and try to find out one thing and accidentally light on another ;* and

5

EGYPTIAN MUMMIES

" (3) Observation of the instincts of living animals : *for example, seeing flies and other insects enclosed in amber may have suggested the idea.*

" *But since these things appear rather fabulous and the pleasant flights of acute wits and inquisitive naturalists than solid truths, we must have recourse to some other course* " ;

and expressed the opinion that—

" *The sands of Egypt being hot, from the reflection of the scorching sun, are capable of preserving bodies without either salination or embalming, and that only by exhaling and drying up the humidities and adventitious moisture, insomuch that it has occasioned no small contests among some authors, which of the two is the truer mummy, that dried in the sands or that which is embalmed with balsams and aromatics.*"

" *The continuance and duration of their embalmings are in some measure due to the clearness and dryness of the air.*"

PREFACE

THERE is nothing more characteristically Egyptian than a mummy, and yet, strange as it may seem, very little has been done to acquire an accurate and reliable knowledge of the technical processes and significance of mummy-making. If the reader take up any general text-book on Egypt at the present day, he will usually find a relatively short space devoted to mummies. Moreover, the account, such as it is, is generally compounded chiefly of extracts from classical writers and of a series of generalisations, many of them quite wrong, which have appeared in book after book in the last fifty years. In 1834, Thomas Pettigrew, a London surgeon, published his *History of Egyptian Mummies*, which, considering the archæological data then at his disposal, is a monument of exact observation. Since that time, however, so far as we are aware, no monograph has appeared based upon the examination of actual mummies and dealing as a whole with the development and significance of Egyptian embalming. In recent years large numbers of mummies of various periods have been examined (and twice as many more allowed to perish without record), and we now have sufficient data to enable us to trace the origin and development of this singular practice over a period of at least three thousand years.

We have aimed merely at tracing in outline the technical processes employed by the embalmer, and at briefly describing the funeral ceremonies and other such archæological

EGYPTIAN MUMMIES

matters directly relating to mummies, but these subjects demand a full treatment which would be out of place in this book. We have touched but lightly on the motives that prompted the custom and of the far-reaching effects it has had in shaping the development of human thought, not only in Egypt, but throughout the world. We have indicated the ancient literature relating to embalming from Egyptian and Greek texts, but as these cannot be intelligibly translated without a philological commentary, we have attempted to convey their meaning rather than their exact words. The geographical distribution of mummification and the story of its spread throughout the world we have not touched upon at all, as the amount of evidence now available for this aspect of the subject would, if set out, have doubled the bulk of this book. These wider questions of the origin and spread of mummification have been dealt with at considerable length elsewhere.[1]

Mummification had a great influence on the development of the science of anatomy, and in fact of medicine in general, and Egyptian mummies themselves have furnished us with so many pathological conditions of the greatest interest in the history of medicine, that a chapter has been devoted to the subject.

For more technical descriptions and for fuller information on the various subjects indicated or discussed, the reader is referred to the footnotes, in which ample bibliographical references will be found.

This book is to be regarded not as a complete treatise so much as a sketch to suggest the far-reaching importance of the study of mummification and to indicate the sort of

---

[1] G. Elliot Smith : *The Migrations of Early Culture* (1915) and *The Evolution of the Dragon* (1919) ; W. J. Perry : *Children of the Sun* (1923), *Origin of Magic and Religion* (1923) and *The Growth of Civilization* (1924).

PREFACE

information that is required to complete the story. It is hoped that it may have some influence in stimulating archæologists to pay more serious attention to the investigation of the subject.

We wish to thank Professor Capart, Director of the Musées Royaux of Brussels, for the photographs from which Figs. 4, 5 and 44 have been reproduced, and Mr. Fred Hall for valuable help in preparing the manuscript.

For the beautiful water-colour sketch from which the Frontispiece has been prepared, we are indebted to Mrs. Cecil Firth.

G. E. S.

LONDON,   W. R. D.

March, 1924.

CONTENTS

APPENDIX

11

ILLUSTRATIONS

Ptolemaic Mummy in Cartonnage Casing   *Frontispiece*

13

EGYPTIAN MUMMIES

14

ILLUSTRATIONS

15

EGYPTIAN MUMMIES

CHAPTER I

INTRODUCTION

OF all the customs of the Ancient Egyptians mummification is surely the most curious and distinctive. Although embalming has been practised in other countries, in some cases for many centuries, the word " mummy " will always connote Egypt and an Egyptian invention,[1] in spite of the fact that in the land where it originated mummification is now unknown, having been finally abandoned more than twelve centuries ago. Considering the great interest that is commonly aroused by this bizarre method for disposal of the dead, there is a curious lack of reference to its origin and development in the literature that has come down to us from ancient times. Most of our knowledge of the inspiration and technique of the embalmer's art has been derived from the application in recent times of modern scientific methods of examination to mummies found during Egyptian excavations. But a few writers of the ancient world were interested to observe the practice of embalming, and have left to posterity records which, although not always exactly reconcilable, are of great value in providing a large measure of contemporary

---

[1] See G. Elliot Smith's *The Migrations of Early Culture*, in which the geographical distribution of mummification is dealt with at length.

support for the conclusions to which modern investigators have been led.

The most instructive of these writers are Herodotus and Diodorus Siculus.[1] In his *Euterpe* Herodotus relates the details of three methods, the first of which could be afforded only by the wealthy, the second being of a more moderate expense, and the third for people of " yet meaner circumstances." Written about four centuries later, that is *circa* 80 B.C., the account of Diodorus gives the relative cost of these preparations : " In the first, they say, there is spent a talent of silver ; in the second twenty minæ ; but in the last there is very little expense." [2] It also provides additional details, not only of the practice of mummification, but also of other funerary rites of the Egyptians, including those by which the dead man was judged, and taken on a boat across a lake, or the Nile, an act emblematical of his voyage to the other-world.[3] Diodorus, moreover, emphasises the importance attached by the Egyptians to the need for the disposal of the dead in accordance with the custom of the time. The strength of their feelings on this subject was due to the religious beliefs bound up with the origins of embalming, and was the cause of the devotion with which the practitioners of the art pursued their experiments over a period of more than three thousand years, in the unceasing effort to attain perfection. Before turning to discuss the question of the origin of mummification, we may notice the names of the few other writers of ancient, mediæval and early modern times who recorded their impressions of that peculiar process. Both Pettigrew, the author of the first adequate

---

[1] See Chapter IV.
[2] See below Chapter IV, where this question is more fully discussed and some other evidence as to cost is adduced.
[3] For the burial ceremonies and their significance see below, Chapter II.

INTRODUCTION

discussion of this subject in England (*History of Egyptian Mummies*, London, 1834), and Dr. Louis Reutter (*L'Embaumement*, Paris, 1912), have been assiduous in collecting such references, but no other accounts that they have found can vie with those of Herodotus and Diodorus for interest and fulness of information. Homer speaks in one place of the use of nectar and ambrosia, which were injected through the nostrils of Patrocles for the purpose of preserving his body, while an account of the encasing in wax of the corpse of Agesilaus, in order that it might be brought to his native land, is given by Emilius Probus, Cornelius Nepos, and Plutarch. According to later writers, also, the body of Alexander the Great was embalmed in honey and conveyed by Ptolemy in a golden coffin to Memphis, where it was exhibited to the wondering gaze of the populace.[1]

The Greek physician Dioscorides discusses the virtues of a substance called in the Latin *mumia*,[2] a black bituminous matter found oozing from the earth in certain places, and down to comparatively recent times the word " mummy " has been used to denote such material. This " mummy " was regarded by the Persians as a panacea for physical ailments, and one of their writers of the tenth century A.D. has left a description of the complicated arrangements made for the safeguarding of the mountain from which this precious exudation was derived, and of the ceremony attaching to its annual collection on behalf of the Shah. A similar description of mummy was made by Abd' al-Latif, an Arab writer of the twelfth century, who was, however, also well acquainted with mummy in the modern sense of that word.[3]

---

[1] In addition to the authorities collected by Pettigrew and others, reference may be made to a curious little treatise entitled *Tractatus de Balsamatione Cadaverum*, by Joseph Lanzoni, published at Geneva in 1696.

[2] *De Materia Medica*, Book I, chap. 100.

[3] Abd' al-Latif, *ed.* de Sacy, p. 200.

EGYPTIAN MUMMIES

This extended use of the term, which was customary until well on in the nineteenth century, was due to the probability that from late Ptolemaic times onwards bituminous materials were largely used in the process of embalming, and the belief became widely prevalent that the wonderful cures originally attributed to the exudation of which we have spoken could also be obtained by the use of fragments of human bodies which had been subjected to this treatment. Most of the references to mummy in early modern times are devoted, therefore, to a discussion of its healing virtues. The earliest use of mummy as a drug is supposed to have been made by a Jewish physician of Alexandria about A.D. 1200. It soon became widespread. Pettigrew gives a number of quotations concerning the merits of mummy for medicinal purposes from writers of the seventeenth and eighteenth centuries, which show that it was well known all over Western Europe. Lord Bacon and Boyle acknowledge its merits, which were also enshrined in various pharmacopœias of the time, but other writers, of whom perhaps the most famous is Ambroise Paré (*Workes*, London, 1634), condemned the use of this " wicked kind of drugge " as being completely inefficacious.

According to Guyon, the disappearance of this medicament was due not to these criticisms, but to the fears entertained by the Jewish merchants of the commodity when it was discovered that they were accustomed to sell any bodies of which they could get possession, after treating them in such a way as to simulate the real Egyptian mummy.[1]

Whatever the real cause, its use ceased, and with it the medical writings that had accompanied its spread. The

---

[1] For a valuable contribution to the study of mummy in medicine see the paper *Mumie als Heilmittel*, by Wiedemann, in the *Zeitschrift . . . für rhinische und westfälische Volkskunde*, 1906, pp. 1–38.

INTRODUCTION

next reappearance of the mummy in literature occurs with the beginnings of modern Egyptology, and especially with the publication of Pettigrew's remarkable work. It is a matter for much regret that the work of excavating and restoring the old Egyptian sites should have been conducted for the most part along narrowly specialised lines. The absence of adequate co-operation between students of particular subjects has led to the loss of much material that would have been invaluable as definite evidence of the ideas and customs of the Ancient Egyptians. Numerous examples could be cited in these pages of such loss of material, already far too scanty for our needs in reconstructing the history of Egyptian civilisation, but the extremely important discovery at the Temple of Deir-el-Bahari of an embalmer's workshop, which was found during the clearing of the great temple, buried for centuries beneath the sands, is perhaps the most regrettable instance. The primary interest of the excavators was Egyptian architecture, and all the information vouchsafed by them respecting the equipment of the workshop is contained in the following passage of their report :—

When the Northern Colonnade was cleared, we found that brick walls had often been built between the columns, forming small cells or chambers. From the remains found in them, consisting of broken beads, fragments of papyri, and pots containing nitre, we gathered that these chambers were occupied by embalmers who dwelt also on the slope outside the temple. There we found, in the second year of our excavations, very clear indications of the presence of such craftsmen. Just above the wall of the Colonnade were several large jars, some of which were filled with chopped straw used for stuffing the mummies, while others contained numbers of little bags of nitre or some salt used in mummification. Among the jars was a very fine coffin, well painted, with the face dark brown. The inscriptions showed that it had been made for a priest of Mentu of the XXIInd Dynasty called Namenkhetamon, who was of high birth, his great-grandfather being King Osorkon I of the XXIInd Dynasty. When the coffin was opened it was found that there was no body inside,

21

but several hundred of little bags full of nitre. It is to be presumed that the coffin was not paid for, or that the purchasers, having changed their minds, had left it, and the embalmers used it for storing their chemicals.[1]

The inadequacy of such treatment is too obvious to need emphasis. But the correlation of the results of research in different fields, rendered unnecessarily laborious by such indifference, has succeeded in throwing a flood of light on features of Egyptian culture that are of profound importance to the proper understanding of the history of ideas. Among all these features the Egyptian mummy stands as a central object round which gather the contributions of the ancients to the development of religion, art, and science. It thus becomes a matter of first importance to account for the origins of an institution which has played so great a part in moulding the civilisations succeeding that in which it flourished.

Egyptian literature is singularly reticent upon the subject of embalming. What little information it affords is set forth in Chapter III; but it is interesting to pay particular attention at the outset to the earliest specific reference to mummification, written perhaps forty centuries ago.

After the VIth Dynasty the power of Egypt began to crumble and the rule of the Pharaoh was disputed by various local chieftains, who also struggled among themselves for the supremacy which they denied to their nominal ruler. The state of chaos that resulted from this anarchy has been graphically depicted in one of the most remarkable documents that have come down from antiquity. This has been interpreted, under the title *Admonitions of an Egyptian Sage*,[2] by Dr. Alan H. Gardiner. Among the afflictions that

[1] Naville: *Deir el Bahari*, pt. ii, p. 6. [2] Leipzig, 1909.

INTRODUCTION

had befallen his country the scribe calls attention to the baneful effects of the interference with foreign intercourse, and specially mentions the inability to obtain from the Lebanons (through its seaport at Byblos) the materials for embalming as one of the direst afflictions produced by the political disturbance.[1]

The scanty references to embalming in the later periods of Egyptian history will be fully discussed in Chapter IV.

There are reasons for the belief that the earliest attempts to prevent the corruption of the body by artificial devices were suggested by the remarkable phenomenon of the natural preservation of the corpses of the dead. In predynastic times in Egypt (i.e. before the commencement of the Ist Dynasty, circa 3400–3100 B.C.) it was the custom to bury the dead, loosely wrapped in linen and skins or matting, in shallow graves ; and the hot dry sand, which, in spite of these coverings, came into direct contact with the skin, often desiccated the body and so arrested the process of decomposition that under less exceptional conditions is its usual fate in the grave. The discovery of the fact that these bodies " did not suffer corruption but had put on incorruption " was probably made known to the early Egyptians as the result of the depredations of jackals in their cemeteries, and especially such human jackals as the grave robber, who plied his nefarious trade even in the earliest known period of man's history in the Nile Valley.[2]

The realisation of the fact of this natural preservation undoubtedly strengthened men's belief in the survival of the dead ; and evidence in substantiation of this intenser faith is afforded by the ampler provision of food and equipment which the Egyptians began to make for the use of the

[1] The passage is translated below, p. 55.
[2] George A. Reisner, Archæological Report (Egypt Exploration Fund), 1900–1901, pp. 23–25.

EGYPTIAN MUMMIES

dead. The time soon arrived when the grave itself had to be made more spacious to accommodate these more abundant supplies of sustenance for the occupant of the grave.

But the burial of the dead in these roomier graves, in which the corpse was no longer in direct contact with the dry sand of the desert but in a chamber filled with air, defeated the very object that had prompted the more lavish equipment. For the natural preservation of the body occurred much less often than in earlier times when it was closely surrounded by the sand. But by this time the desirability of preventing the corruption of the body had become firmly fixed as a cardinal article of the faith that preservation of the body was the essential factor in securing a continuance of existence. Hence the Egyptians began to experiment with the object of discovering some means of achieving by art what unaided nature rarely effected in the larger tombs.

If this hypothesis represents a true picture of the trend of Egyptian thoughts and aspirations—and the available evidence points so definitely to these conclusions that there is little room for doubt as to the accuracy of this inference— such attempts at mummification were in all probability made when the Egyptians first realised the results of burial in larger tombs. On these grounds it may confidently be assumed that the first experiments were made approximately at the commencement of the Ist Dynasty. As we have concrete evidence of such attempts at the time of the IInd Dynasty (Fig. 1), the inference as to the date of origin of the practice of mummification is virtually confirmed.

Long before the attempt was made to embalm human bodies the Egyptians were familiar with the more obvious properties of the materials which they subsequently used as preservatives. For many centuries resins had been used as one of the ingredients for making cosmetics (Fig. 2);

INTRODUCTION

and in some of the earliest mummies that have been spared for us to study (Fig. 3) this substance was liberally used. In the deserts fringing the habitable land in the valley, both in Upper and Lower Egypt, salt and soda are found in vast quantities, and as both of these substances were used by the embalmer even in the earliest times, we have positive evidence that their properties must have been familiar to the inventors of the art of embalming.

From the time of their first attempts the embalmers kept before them two objects, from which their attention never swerved until Egypt's might crumbled before the power of Islam thousands of years later. The first of these, as has been indicated, was to *prevent decomposition of the tissues of the body*, and the second was the *preservation of the living form and personal identity of the individual*.[1] The constant striving after this second object is the explanation, not only of the exceptional trouble taken by the embalmers in treating the head, but also of many of the inscriptions found on the walls of the tombs, all of which were intended to ensure the identification of the departed with Osiris. Just as the discovery of the natural preservation of the body had crystallised the vague aspirations of the earliest Egyptian into a faith in personal immortality, so did the practice of mummification transform this belief, so that it acquired the definition and intensity of a vital creed. Embalming thus became the essential feature of the religious and philosophical edifice that grew up around it and that has persisted through the ages, under varying forms, since first it seemed to offer men the possibility of attaining immunity from extinction. How vast an influence the practice of mummification exerted upon the shaping of the nascent religious beliefs in the times of the earliest civilisations has recently

[1] See *Journal of Egyptian Archæology*, vol. i, pp. 189 ff.

been demonstrated in a novel way by Mr. W. J. Perry in his book on *The Origin of Magic and Religion* (p. 68). Contrasting the earliest beliefs of Egypt, Sumer, and Crete, he finds that in the two latter (where embalming was not practised in early times) there is no trace of the conception of immortality such as was being shaped in Egypt in close correlation with the ideas suggested by the practices for rendering the body imperishable and everlasting.

In the earliest phase of the embalmers' experiments the bodies were wrapped in a series of linen bandages, and such attempts as were made to render the individual recognisable were carried out on the swathed mummy, with the object of making it also a portrait statue of the deceased. The difficulty of securing life-like results by these means soon became apparent to the Egyptians, who therefore resorted to other methods of preserving the likeness of the departed, and thereby, as was believed, of securing the continuance of his existence. Their first device was the making, out of limestone or Nile mud, of a model of the dead man's head, which was placed with his mummy in the burial chamber. This development took place during the Pyramid Age (IVth Dynasty), and at about the same time death masks were also introduced.[1] While the latter custom never attained any great importance, the making of a portrait model of the head was developed until eventually a statue of the whole body was modelled. This statue was supposed to become the habitation of the " Ka "—one of the twin souls of the dead—while the other (" Bai ") passed to the

---

[1] See Junker, *Journ. Eg. Arch.*, vol. i, p. 252 and Pl. XL, and Reisner, *Bull. Boston Mus. of Fine Arts*, vol. xiii, No. 76, April 1915, where pictures and descriptions of the " substitute heads " will be found. For Egyptian death masks see Quibell, *Excavations at Saqqara* 1907–8, p. 113, and Petrie, *Tell el Amarna*, Pl. I. See also Elliot Smith, *Evolution of the Dragon*, pp. 16 ff.

INTRODUCTION

other world to become deified in identification with Osiris. The significant place in the Egyptian system occupied by the portrait statue is revealed by the names used for the sculptor—" he who causes to live "—and for the act of making such a statue, which is the same as the Egyptian word meaning " to give birth," [1] the idea being that the modelling of a life-like portrait was in fact the creation of a living image, a perpetuation of the life of the deceased, in other words a rebirth or renewal of life. But it is worthy of note that this development never deterred the embalmers from their efforts to preserve in the mummy itself the actual lineaments of the dead. Many centuries later they satisfied themselves of their ability to achieve this aim, but during the intervening period the statue contributed much to the consolidation of their ritual and beliefs.

Some of its outstanding influences should be noticed, because of their reverberations throughout the history of religion. With the invention of the statue proper arose the custom of housing it in a chamber on the surface of the earth as an efficient animate representative of the body it duplicated, which lay at rest, safely hidden away in a subterranean vault. To the statue in its own apartment were made the periodical offerings of food, incense and libations, and the animating ceremonies that were thought to be necessary for the continuance of the existence of the dead man. The offerings of incense and libations were of particular importance, inasmuch as they were intended to restore to the corpse those vital odours and moisture the absence of which was the most conspicuous difference between the mummy and the living person.[2] Ignorant as they were of the physiological aspects of life and death, it

[1] See Capart, *Egyptian Art*, London, 1923, p. 173.
[2] See below, Chapter II, where this subject is fully discussed (pp. 35–37).

27

seemed to them the obvious course to pursue, to give back to the body of the dead such attributes of life as were not present in the corpse. The absence of bodily odour and of moisture they sought to overcome by the use of incense and the pouring out of libations before the mummy or the statue. Similarly, the mouth was opened to restore to it the breath of life, and the reanimation of the dead was attempted by the performance of dramatic action in the tomb. When these ceremonies had been executed it was supposed that the dead monarch continued his existence, and that as, during his reign, he had been the guardian of the realm, so would his reincarnation continue to protect and guide his successors in the task of government. As already suggested, these rites were periodically repeated in the case of every individual king. At first the reigning king would be responsible for the maintenance in due season of the celebrations on which depended the immortality of his ancestors. In course of time the combined demands of religion and of government inevitably became so onerous as to necessitate separation, and when this was realised the way was clear for the emergence, for the first time, of a professional priesthood. This differentiation of function produced further reaction upon the religious structure. The offering of food, incense, and libations was originally made in the precincts of the tomb itself for the purpose of providing " life " to the departed. But with the growing elaboration of the tombs and the growth of a priestly caste, over a long period of time, this original intention was over-shadowed by a new conception of the rites as an act of worship of the deified dead. When this new idea had taken root in the minds of men the previously essential identity of the place of worship with the tomb was forgotten. Hence the practice arose of conducting religious ceremonies in a temple that might be far removed from the spot in

INTRODUCTION

which the bodies that prompted such ritual acts lay enshrined. Such was the origin of places of worship, not
merely of ancient but also of modern times.

To the same course of development may also be ascribed
the beginning of the practice of setting up " graven images "
as deities. The Kings of Egypt, for whose sole benefit
mummification was originally devised, were regarded (after
the IVth Dynasty) as beings of divine descent—Sons of
the Sun. The portrait statues set up to each of them as
the habitation of the "Ka" was thus itself an embodiment of
godhead, and the separation of temple and tomb made it easy
for the laymen at least to overlook its representative character, and to come to consider it as a divinity which was
in itself a fit object of worship.

All these are indications of the way in which the long
process of the consolidation of Egyptian culture affected
the subsequent development of civilisation. Similar influences were brought to bear on the more material elements
of culture. Two of the arts which derived their first inspiration from the practice of mummification have already
been indicated. Elaboration of the tombs was the main-
spring of architectural progress under the Pharaohs, which
was characterised by the use of stone and the development
of the technique of masonry, while the making of portrait
statues as a means of securing immortality provided the
first powerful incentive to the life-like reproduction of the
human form in statuary. Similarly the art of fine woodwork
was developed from the making of coffins, the use of which
was evolved during the series of changes and custom which
ultimately brought about the substitution of entombment
for inhumation. In his recent address to the British Association at Liverpool, Professor Percy E. Newberry criticised
the claim that the Egyptians invented the crafts of the
carpenter and the shipbuilder on the ground that suitable

timber was lacking in Egypt. But the evidence in demonstration of the fact that they did really devise these practices is clear and definite. Professor Reisner's excavations at Naga ed Dêr in Upper Egypt reveal every stage in the gradual development in the use of local wood; and it is patent that it was the empirical knowledge so acquired that prompted the Egyptians to search for and import better timber from abroad. This they did by means of ships built in imitation (not merely in shape, but also in method of construction) of the papyrus floats devised for use on the Nile. Similarly the fundamental importance of their burial customs to the Egyptians led to the conscious improvement and elaboration, in the interests of the dead, of metal work, jewellery, and ceramics, superb examples of which have been found in the royal tombs, and especially in that of Tutankhamen, which is unique in having been found almost intact.

Such reflections as these make for a readier acknowledgment than is usually accorded of the great part played in history by Egypt, and of the significance of the mummy as the synthesising factor in our understanding of that rôle. But there is a further consideration to be borne in mind, the importance of which lies in the evidence it affords that this ancient influence has not been confined to the world known to the Pharaohs, but has been extended and expanded until there is hardly a spot in the world as we now know it that does not bear in its own culture some trace of the earliest of civilisations. The reasons for the origin of mummification in Egypt we have seen. The close relationship subsisting between this practice and the use of stone, both for constructing tombs and temples, and for the erection of statues, is also easily apparent. But when we think of the general characteristics of Egyptian arts and beliefs, all closely moulded by the peculiar conditions of the valley of the Nile, we find scores of other unrelated elements welded by the most fortuitous circumstances into a unique whole that could have been evolved in no other part of the world. The worship of the sun and the serpent, the use of the symbols of the winged disk, the complicated myths of the creation of the world and of man's destruction by a universal deluge, such curious practices as tattooing, artificial deformation of the head and " couvade," these are but a few of the many elements that entered into the cultural complex of Ancient Egypt. When, therefore, in examining the civilisations of other races and other periods, we find all over the world the same concatenation of these and many other elements that are distinctively Egyptian in character, we are constrained to recognise the fact of the widespread diffusion of that ancient culture. And to relate this conclusion more closely to the mummy which so largely conditioned its shape, it may be pointed out that the practice of mummification itself has had a distribution extending from Asia Minor southwards into the African interior, westwards into Europe, and eastwards, by way of India, Burma and Indo-China to New Guinea and the islands of the Pacific, whence it spread to Peru and permeated Central America,[1] while Egyptian literature examined by Dr. Blackman makes it certain that the use of incense and libations originated out of the practice of embalming, so that in every part of the world where these customs are observed we have indirect evidence of the influence of Egyptian ideas.

Thus we see that the cultural structures of races in every continent of the globe have owed parts either of their formative inspiration, or of the elements entering into them,

---

[1] Elliot Smith : *The Migrations of Early Culture.*

to the genius of the remote past in Egypt. It is in the light of this. realisation that we must seek understanding of the full significance of that genius in world affairs, and the importance of the study of the mummy as its most vital expression.

FIG. I.——THE EARLIEST BODY, AS YET KNOWN, EXHIBITING AN ATTEMPT
AT MUMMIFICATION. IInd DYNASTY

(From Mr. Quibell's photograph of the body *in situ* in the broken coffin)

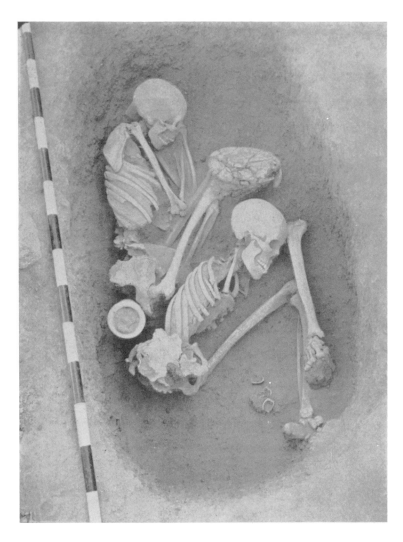

FIG. 2.—PREDYNASTIC BODIES WITH A LARGE CAKE OF RESIN *IN SITU* IN THE GRAVE

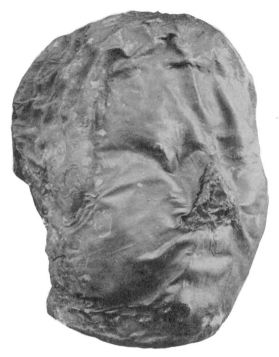

FIG. 3.——HEAD OF A MUMMY, PROBABLY OF THE Vth DYNASTY
(Now in the Museum of the Royal College of Surgeons, London)

FIG. 4.—EGYPTIAN FUNERAL PROCESSION ; FROM THE THEBAN TOMB OF HAREMHAB. XVIIIth DYNASTY

CHAPTER II

THE DEATH AND BURIAL OF AN EGYPTIAN

A S the mummy was the central figure in the complex and elaborate ceremonies enacted at the funeral of an Egyptian and was the host and occupant of the tomb, a brief account must be given of the rites which were performed after the embalmers' work was finished and the wrapped and coffined mummy ready for the tomb.

It must be remembered that the whole funerary cult of the Egyptians was originally intended only for the King, and it was the result of a gradual democratisation of religious ideas [1] that it was borrowed during the old kingdom for nobles and for the highest officials, extending more and more as time went on, and percolating to other and lower ranks of the population, but its kingly origin was never forgotten and traces of it reappear again and again, as we shall presently see.

By his death and embalming, and by virtue of the magical and religious ceremonies enacted in connexion therewith, the dead man became identified with Osiris, the dead King *par excellence*, and he went through, in theory at least, all the phases that befel the god after his fatal conflict with Seth.

For the purposes of this description, we will take the burial of an Egyptian noble of the New Kingdom, a period

---

[1] This democratisation is admirably worked out by Breasted in his *Development of Religion and Thought in Ancient Egypt*.

EGYPTIAN MUMMIES

when the funerary cult had reached its greatest elaboration. The account is therefore mainly based upon the Theban Tomb of Amenemhēt, not only because it is a good representative of its class, but because it is the subject of an admirable memoir to which reference is continually made throughout this book, to which we cannot adequately express our indebtedness, and which is far and away the best exposition published on Egyptian funerary ceremonies.[1]

We know very little of what immediately followed the physical death of an Egyptian. The death-bed is a scene never represented as far as we are aware, but an Old Kingdom tomb portrays very vividly the sudden death of a noble who collapses on the ground in the midst of his family whose grief is unmistakably depicted, whilst his wife, overcome by emotion, swoons into the arms of two attendants.[2] In the Royal Tomb at Tell-el-Amarna the death and mourning of a princess is depicted. From the day of death to the completion of the burial rites the usual period of time was seventy days, during which the corpse was handed over

---

[1] *The Theban Tombs Series*, vol. i.   *The Tomb of Amenemhēt* (No. 82), copied in line and colour by Nina de Garis Davies, with explanatory text by Alan H. Gardiner, D.Litt.   London, 1915.

Amongst the other Theban Tombs utilised in this chapter the following may be mentioned as the principal sources :—

The Tomb of Rekhmirē (No. 100).   Virey : *Mém. Miss. Arch.*, t. v, fasc. 1.

The Tomb of Haremhab (No. 78).   Bouriant : *idem.*, fasc. 2, pp. 413–434.

The Tomb of Neferhotpe (No. 50).   Benedite : *idem.* fasc. 2, pp. 489–540.

The Tomb of Antefoker (No. 60) (Middle Kingdom).   Davies : *The Tomb of Antefoker and his Wife Senet.*   London, 1920.

The five tombs (Nos. 20, 21, 103, 165, 154) published by Davies in his *Five Theban Tombs*, London 1913, have also been used.

The Tomb of Paheri at El Kab (early XVIIIth Dynasty) is also often quoted. See Griffith-Tylor : *The Tomb of Paheri* (Egypt Expl. Fund, XIth Memoir), 1894.

(The numbers of the tombs refer to those in Gardiner and Weigall, *Topographical Catalogue of the Private Tombs of Thebes*, London 1913.)

[2] Bissing : *Denkmäler Aeg. Sculptur*, Pl. 18B, quoted by Gardiner, *op. cit.* p. 45, note 1.   Reproduced also in Capart : *Rue de Tombeaux*, Pl. LXXI.

BURIAL OF AN EGYPTIAN

to the embalmers, whose finished product was the bandaged mummy ready to receive the last rites from earthly ministrants before its consignment to the depths of the tomb.[1] The embalmers' workshop was called the *House of Purification of the Good House,* and in it a long and complicated series of rites was enacted during the wrapping of the mummy and the placing of its amulets in their places.[2] The details of the actual process of mummification will be fully described in the later chapters which describe mummies of various periods ; [3] for the present it will suffice to say that the body was first eviscerated, soaked in a salt-bath, and finally anointed and wrapped in its complex clothing of bandages.[4]

Throughout all these ceremonies, and also those which followed, libations were poured out and incense burnt. The significance of incense and libations, to which reference was made in Chapter I, has been subjected to a careful study by Blackman, who in a series of illuminating memoirs has traced the origin and purpose of this aspect of the funerary ritual.[5] Blackman has shown that these ceremonies imparted to the body the moisture and warmth which it had lost during the process of mummification, and also was the means by which the sun-god was reborn daily and by which the inert corpse of Osiris was revivified. It is in this latter aspect that its significance in the funerary ceremonies is most important. The Osirian lustrations were

---

[1] For the period see Chapter III and where the *Ritual of Embalming* is also discussed.

[2] For the amulets and the texts relating thereto see pp. 147–153.

[3] See Chapters V–VIII.

[4] Pictures of the wrapping and decoration of mummies are rare, but a good instance may be seen in Maspero, *Struggle of the Nations,* 2nd. ed., pp. 510 and 511, reproduced from Rossellini.

[5] *Zeitschrift fur Ägyptische Sprache,* t. 50, pp. 69 ff. *Journal of Egyptian Archæology,* t. v, pp. 118–124 and 148–165. *Proceedings of the Society of Biblical Archæology,* t. xl, pp. 57–66 and 86–91. *Recueil de Travaux,* t. 39, pp. 44–78. See also Elliot-Smith : *Evolution of the Dragon,* chap. i.

performed with water obtained from the mythical source of the Nile (the Island of Bigeh), where a dismembered leg of the god was deposited, and the water was regarded as its sacred emanation. The body of Osiris had been dismembered at his death and his limbs scattered throughout the cities of Egypt. They were afterwards collected and his body was made whole and embalmed and became revivified by the magical power of Isis and other divinities.[1] Consequently the formulæ recited during the lustration of the Osirian dead often speak of the corpse as though it were dismembered like that of Osiris. Thus the lector-priest, during the washing of the dead body of Dhut-hotpe in his tomb at El Bersheh, recites the words : " Unite to thee thy bones : what appertains to thee is complete." [2]

In his article in the *Recueil de Travaux* already cited, which is the authority for the above statements, the author has collected all the known instances of the dead undergoing lustration in the embalmers' workshop.[3] The dead man, who is visualised as living,[4] and represented as fully clothed, stands upon a large pan or squats over a large jar whilst two or more lustrators pour water over him. Blackman suggests with great probability that the jar or vessel beneath the body is to catch the moisture which drains therefrom after its removal from the salt-bath, which would thus have contained a quantity of matter exuded from the body (*op. cit.* p. 55). Whilst the life-giving lustration water mingled with it as it flowed into the jar the dead man

---

[1] For a useful collection of data on the myth of Osiris we have frequently consulted Budge, *Osiris and the Egyptian Resurrection*, 2 vols., London, 1911, although we cannot always accept his conclusions.

[2] Blackman : *Journ. Eg. Arch.*, t. v, p. 119. Newberry : *El Bersheh*, t. i, Pl. X.

[3] *Recueil de Travaux*, t. 39, pp. 53–55 and Pl. III. To these must be added the corresponding scene in the Tomb of Amenhotpe-si-se, published in vol. iii of the *Theban Tombs Series*, Pl. XV (1924).

[4] See Dawson : " A Rare Vignette from the Book of the Dead," in *Journ. Eg. Arch.*, vol. x, pt. i. p. 40.

would be revivified with these potent emanations, which by his identification with Osiris became the emanations from the god of the potency of which the religious texts of all periods from the Pyramid Age to Roman times speak again and again.

This interpretation is of special importance in view of the discoveries made from time to time in the Theban necropolis of piles of pots filled with rags and salt which are, as Mr. H. E. Winlock states, " the refuse of embalmers' shops." His report of the finding of such deposits is of such interest that we make no apology for quoting the following extracts from it : [1]

This year alone we ran across three such caches of the later periods, and two years ago we found the same sort of things left over from the embalming of the body of Mehenkwetre. A little chamber had been provided for them near the tomb because they had been in contact with the dead man's body and therefore contained some of the essence of his being, but outside of the courtyard because all that appertained to embalming was essentially impure.[2] That chamber had been entered before our day, but this year we found the similar chamber of the tomb of Ipy just as it had been sealed up after his funeral, and some of the things in it were, so far as we know, unique. . . . The great noble had provided for the embalming of his body most liberally. Cloths, salts, aromatic oils, sawdust and countless pottery vessels, far beyond ordinary requirements, were laid aside against the day of his death. In addition a wooden platform 7 ft. 1 in. long and 4 ft. 2½ in. wide was prepared with four wooden blocks of ghastly similarity to those on the dissecting tables of modern medical schools. . . . Then, after the embalming was completed and Ipy's mummy duly wrapped in its bandages, all that had touched it was gathered up religiously for the possession of so much as a hair of his head by an enemy would provide the means of bewitching him. Soiled rags, broken pots, left-over salts . . . were packed in sixty-seven large jars, which were sealed and carried up to the little chamber by the tomb.[3]

---

[1] " The Egyptian Expedition MCMXXI–MCMXXII," part ii of the *Bulletin of the Metropolitan Museum of Art*, New York, December 1922, p. 34.

[2] We cannot agree with this interpretation, as all the facts as well as the Egyptian texts, seem to prove just the reverse. The emanations of the corpse, being assimilated to Osiris, were the essence of the god himself, which were therefore doubly sacred and abundantly treated as such in innumerable religious texts.   [3] *Op. cit.* p. 34.

EGYPTIAN MUMMIES

Some of these jars still lie in the rope sling-nets in which they were carried. Two similar sets of jars in sling-nets and hung upon poles for carrying were found in the tomb of, and lying beside, a XVIIth Dynasty mummy at Qurneh by Petrie,[1] which had doubtless served a similar purpose, and other instances might be quoted.

Although the lustration of the body and the vessels used in connexion herewith is of the greatest importance and contains many of the foundation-stones of Egyptian funerary ideas, it cannot be further elaborated now. Enough, however, has been said to show that these rites, like all the others connected with burial customs, were a dramatic re-enaction of the embalming and burial of Osiris, in which the dead man played the part of the god and his priestly ministrants played the parts of the gods who assisted at the obsequies of Osiris.

We will now turn our attention to the funeral procession which set out from the dead man's house and accompanied him to the tomb. (Fig. 4.)

A frequently depicted episode is the journey to Abydos (Fig. 4, lowest register). Like many of the other episodes, the scene is easy to describe but difficult to explain. The dead man and his wife sit under a canopy in a state barge towed by a boat with two rows of oarsmen. The barge is accompanied by others on which the priests perform sacrifices and rites as the journey proceeds. Whatever its original purpose may have been, all the evidence seems to point to the fact which Gardiner has brought out so well,[2]— that the journey at least in the New Kingdom, if not earlier,[3] had no objective reality, but was replaced by a mere pictorial

---

[1] Petrie : *Qurneh*, pp. 6 ff. and Pl. XXIV.
[2] Gardiner : *op. cit.* p. 48.
[3] Davies : *Tomb of Antefoker*, p. 19.

representation on the tomb walls. The procession had to cross the Nile, or at least some of its rites were performed on the water, and in many tombs these aquatic incidents and the journey to Abydos are all placed together. The shrine, the coffin and the mourners are shown in light papyrus skiffs on the water. A curious survival of the times when the burial rites were exclusive to kings is the frequent representation of statues, usually two in number, wearing the Red Crown of the Pharaoh. These are generally carried at the head of the procession of servants bearing tomb furniture.[1] They are also shown on the boats, usually with a sacrificial joint laid before them by an officiating priest.[2]

The simplest representations of the funeral procession and ceremonies are those which illustrate the funerary papyri (*Book of the Dead*) of the XVIIIth, XIXth and XXth Dynasties.[3] These show the hearse, the mourners, the servants bearing furniture, and the final rites before the mummy at the door of the tomb. The pictures in the tombs go into much greater detail, and display a great amount of variation. The order of the procession is not always the same but the stamp of a common tradition pervades all the pictures.

Sepulchral stelæ sometimes give summarised versions of the funeral ceremonies. The stela C 15 is a very remarkable

---

[1] *Rekhmirē*, Pls. XIX and XXII ; *Antefoker*, Pl. XXI. In the Tomb of *Haremhab*, these two figures are represented by busts, like that found in the Tomb of Tutankhamen, but wearing the wig head-dress instead of crowns. Royal crowns are frequently included amongst the burial equipment of non-royal persons on coffins of the Middle Kingdom, and amongst groups of such objects in the tombs of the New Kingdom. For the former see Lacau : *Sarcophages anterieurs au Nouvel Empire*, t. ii, Pl. LIV ; and for the latter, Bouriant : *Tombeau de Harmhabi*, Pl. V.

[2] *Rekhmirē*, Pls. XIX and XX. *Antefoker*, Pl. XVIII.

[3] E.g. the Papyri of Any, Henufer, etc., or in a still briefer form, Naville, *Papyrus of Iouiya*, Pl. II.

example. (See Fig. 5, reproduced by permission of the authorities of the Louvre Museum.)

The whole procession moves westward towards a figure of the goddess of the West, who wears her characteristic emblems upon her head. The mummy lies in a shrine or canopy upon a lion-headed bier, the whole being placed upon a sledge drawn by oxen and by men.[1] In some cases the outer sarcophagus is placed in the shrine with the mummy on its bier above it, and in other cases the sarcophagus is carried separately.[2] Two women, impersonating Isis and Nephthys, precede the mummy, either on the sledge or on foot.[3] The two goddesses are called the " great kite " and the " little kite," and are sometimes replaced by figures of birds. Behind the hearse another sledge drawn by men follows. This bears, usually on a couch and in a canopy, a coffer, doubtless the chest containing the four canopic jars in which the separately embalmed viscera are deposited.[4] In some cases the canopic box is omitted, and the four jars are placed under the bier in the hearse.[5] Parties of mourning women with bare breasts and dishevelled hair follow the coffin, giving vent to their grief.[6] Next in order comes a procession of servants bearing chests full of clothing,[7] ornaments and other property for the tomb. The objects

[1] The shrine is sometimes closed and conceals the mummy (*Haremhab, Rekhmirē*), but is more often open (*Amenemhēt, Antefoker*). The shrine also often stands upon a boat, which in its turn is carried on the sledge (*Haremhab, Rekhmirē*). In some cases there is neither bier nor boat, and in some scenes the sledge itself is lion-headed (*Mentuherkhepeshef*, etc.).

[2] See Griffith-Tylor : *Tomb of Paheri*, Pl. V. The coffin is carried separately over the river (*Paheri, Antefoker*), or on the shoulders of the bearers on land (*Antefoker*).

[3] On the sledge more often. On foot in *Paheri*.

[4] The Canopic Box was often fitted with runners and combined the box and sledge in one unit, e.g. Quibell : *Tomb of Yuaa and Thuiu*, Pls. XIV and XV.

[5] E.g. *Papyrus of Henufer*.

[6] *Papyrus of Ani*, Pls. V and VI.

[7] In the Tomb of *Haremhab* the servants precede the hearse.

FIG. 5 —THE STELA NO. C. 15 OF THE LOUVRE
(Photo by Professor J. Capart, reproduced by permission of
the authorities of the Louvre Museum)

PIG. 6.—AN XIth DYNASTY MUMMY FROM DEIR-EL-BAHARI—
THE PRINCESS HENHENIT

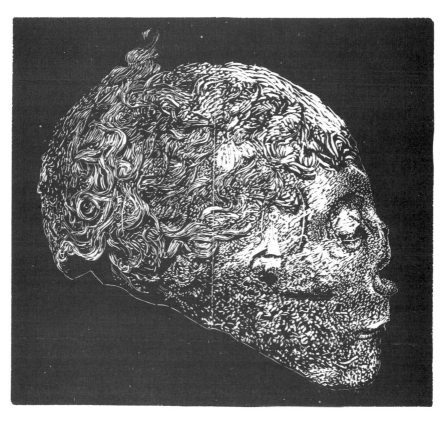

FIG. 7.—HEAD OF THE MUMMY OF THE PHARAOH AAHMOSIS I.
(XVIIIth DYNASTY)

FIG. 8.—HEAD OF THE LADY RAY (EARLY XVIIIth DYNASTY)

BURIAL OF AN EGYPTIAN

contained in these chests are usually depicted above them, and are of the same nature as those depicted upon the coffins of the Middle Kingdom.[1]

A frequent but very obscure feature of the funeral procession is the figure of a man wrapped in an ox-hide and huddled up or crouching upon a sledge drawn by four men. This is called the *tekenu*, but what its origin or function may be is entirely obscure.[2] The figure is usually completely covered in the hide, and appears as a pear-shaped object upon the sledge [3] (Fig. 4, first register). In some cases the head is uncovered,[4] and in one tomb, that of Mentuherkhepeshef, the *tekenu* plays a more obtrusive part, and is quite exceptional both in pose and function.[5]

The long and complex series of pictures which in the tombs we have so frequently referred to, as well as in many others, deal with an entirely obscure series of rites, the meaning and purpose of which we can do little more than guess at. As so often in these pages, we can only refer to the admirable account of them in the *Tomb of Amenemhēt*.[6]

The procession has now arrived at the entrance of the tomb, and the mummy is taken from the hearse and placed upright upon a mound of sand facing the mourners. The rites now to be performed are magical in character and have for their object the transformation of the mummy from an inert corpse to a living being capable of performing all its

---

[1] See Lacau : *Sarcophages anterieurs au Nouvel Empire*, Pls. XXX–LIV.

[2] See Davies : *Tomb of Antefoker*, Pl. XXIIa and p. 22 with footnote 1. Gardiner : *op. cit.*, pp. 50, 51. Moret : *Mystères Égyptiens*, pp. 42 ff.

[3] *Haremhab, Paheri, Amenemhēt, Neferrenpit* (Brussels).

[4] *Antefoker, Rekhmirē.*

[5] Davies : *Five Theban Tombs*, pp. 9, 10, 14.

[6] Pp. 52–57, and especially 55. For the corresponding scenes in other tombs we may mention :—

Paheri, Pl. V ; *Rekhmirē*, Pls. XIX–XXVIII ; *Five Theban Tombs*, Pls. II, VI–X and XXI.

EGYPTIAN MUMMIES

bodily functions in the life of the next world. These ceremonies were very long and complex, and are known as *The Opening of the Mouth*. In the Royal Tombs they are depicted at great length and comprise a long series of episodes. In the private tombs, however, only an abstract is usually given, although even this abstract may comprise a considerable number of episodes.

In ancient times it appears that the ceremonies of *Opening the Mouth* were performed upon a statue of the dead man, but in the New Kingdom the mummy itself takes the place of the statue, except in the case of kings, when the statue is retained. Wooden statues of several of the kings of the XVIIIth and XIXth Dynasties have been found, the finest specimens of which are the two discovered in the Tomb of Tutankhamen, which retained their gold ornaments and insignia.[1] In the Tomb of Rekhmirē all the ceremonies are performed upon a statue of the dead man clad in a long white kilt and holding a staff, instead of upon his mummy. The reason for this may possibly be that the mummy itself was inaccessible, for this tomb contains no burial chamber, the body having been laid to rest elsewhere.

Whether represented by his mummy or by a statue, the deceased stands upon a mound of sand prescribed by ritual, and several different priests carry out the ceremonies. These comprise censing and lustration, the sacrifice of an ox, and the touching of the mouth, jaws and eyes with magical instruments which restored to them their functions. A

---

[1] Coloured pictures of the statues of Tutankhamen have been published in *Wonders of the Past*, Part I, pp. 19 and 20. The statue of Sety I, which is depicted on the walls of his tomb undergoing the ceremonies of *Opening the Mouth*, is in the British Museum (*Guide to the Egyptian Galleries* [*Sculpture*] p. 158, No. 567, 1909). A similar statue of Amenophis II was found in the tomb of that king.

42

BURIAL OF AN EGYPTIAN

frequently depicted but very obscure episode is the awakening of the *sem*-priest, who lies huddled up upon a couch under an ox-skin in an attitude recalling that of the *tekenu*, to which we have already alluded, and with which it may possibly have some connexion. One of the priests impersonates Horus and is called the " Beloved Son," yet another instance of the fact that the whole of the ritual is reminiscent of the passion of Osiris. Other priests proceed to anoint and clothe the dead man and the rite terminates with a banquet, the prescribed *menu* for which is set out at length on the walls of the tomb.

The whole ceremony is of very ancient origin; it is mentioned in the Pyramid Texts of the Vth and VIth Dynasties and appears in tombs of even earlier date.[1]

After the completion of these ceremonies the mourners are entertained at a sumptuous feast, and whilst they eat and drink they are entertained by musicians and dancers, who sing to the accompaniment of harps and other instruments the praises of the dead man, or songs treating of life and death. Of these songs the two most famous are those in the Tomb of Neferhotpe and of one of the Antef Kings, a copy of which is preserved in a papyrus in the British Museum.[2] Meanwhile the mummy has been lowered into the burial chamber together with all its equipment, and a priest wearing a mask and impersonating Anubis gives the finishing touches to the arrangements. Another priest, impersonating Thoth, is the last to leave the chamber, and he drags along the ground a kind of broom made of the

---

[1] For a full description see the great work of Schiaparelli : *Il Libro dei Funerali*, 3 vols., Turin 1882–1890. Budge : *The Book of Opening the Mouth*. 2 vols., 1909. Maspero : *Études de Mythologie, etc.*, vol. i, pp. 283–324, Gardiner : *op. cit.* pp. 57 ff. ; and for the scenes, see the Theban tombs already quoted and Lefebure : *Le Tombeau de Seti I*, pt. iii, Pls. II–XII, and numerous papyri of the New Kingdom, such as those of *Any*, *Henufer*, etc.

[2] *Egyptian Hieratic Papyri, Second Series*, Pls. XLV and XLVI (1923).

EGYPTIAN MUMMIES

hdn-plant. This act is perhaps to banish all evil spirits from the chamber, and to delete from the sand with which the floor is sprinkled all footprints, and thus ensure its integrity.[1]

Such, in briefest outline, are the principal events at an Egyptian funeral. The material is almost unlimited, and almost every tomb presents variations in detail. Some of them introduce innovations, others are archaic and show the ceremonies in earlier stages of development, but all bear the stamp of a common tradition. For full information the reader is referred to the various works cited in the foot-notes. These references by no means supply a complete bibliography, but aim at nothing more than a reference to the most accessible and reliable publications in which fuller details and bibliographical notes abound.

---

[1] This rite is called " Bringing the Foot " and may possibly mean " Removing the Footprint." See the discussion of the rite by Gardiner, *op. cit.* pp. 93, 94, where numerous instances of its occurrence are quoted.

For the arrangement of the burial chamber and the objects therein, see Gardiner, *op. cit.* pp. 110–118.

CHAPTER III

EGYPTIAN TEXTS RELATING TO EMBALMING

THE Egyptian texts relating to embalming are few in number. It is strange that a nation which has bequeathed to posterity such a large mass of documents on every variety of subject should have so little information to impart on the most characteristic and specialised feature of its elaborate funerary cult. It is true that the *Pyramid Texts*, the *Coffin Texts* and the *Book of the Dead* are full of allusions to Osirian myth and to such rites as incense-burning and lustration, which became inextricably interwoven therewith, and similar allusions occur in many mythological and magical texts. The following are all that are known to us as having any direct dealings with any part of the ceremonies of embalming.

1. *The Ritual of Embalming.*—This text has come down to us in two papyri : one in the Cairo Museum [1] (*Pap. Boulaq, No.* 3), the other in the Louvre [2] (*No.* 5158). Both are of late period (Roman) and are contemporary ; they are copied, if not by the same scribe, at least from the same original.[3] They are written in the characteristic hieratic script of the period, but from the mythological and other

---

[1] Mariette : *Les Papyrus égyptiens du Musée du Boulaq*, Paris 1871, t. i.

[2] Deveria : *Catalogue des Manuscrits égyptiens du Louvre*, Paris 1881, pp. 168, 169. Maspero : *Mémoire sur quelques Papyrus du Louvre*, Paris 1878, pp. 14–104 and 2 plates.

[3] For evidence as to this see Maspero : *op. cit.* p. 16.

data they contain it would seem that they are a late redaction of an older book, or at least embody older ideas.

The text contained in these two manuscripts is, unfortunately, far from complete. The Cairo text consists of the last ten pages of a work whose first part is entirely lost, but we have no means of estimating how many pages are missing. Of these ten pages, the first is so badly damaged as to be useless, the second has lost the beginning of most of the lines, but the remaining eight are in good preservation. The Paris text duplicates the last two pages.

The ritual may be divided into two headings : (i) a series of directions to the officiant as to acts to be performed by him upon the mummy ; (ii) prayers and incantations to be recited after each of such acts. The book is essentially a religious one, and not a handbook on embalming for the use of Egyptian priests. It contains no directions relating to, nor indeed any mention of, the technical details of embalming. It prescribes the use and application of various unguents, amulets and bandages to be applied to the body after it has been eviscerated and taken out of the salt-bath. Perhaps when entire it contained directions as to the anointing and wrapping of the whole body, but what remains of it relates to the head (§§ i, ii, vii, viii, ix and x), the back (§§ iii, iv and v), the hands (§§ vi and xi), and the arms, legs and feet (§ xii).

We are now concerned only with the directions themselves and will entirely disregard the incantations, although the latter constitute the greater part of the work. As far as we are aware, there is no complete translation extant other than the admirable pioneer study by Maspero,[1] which embodies a full translation and an elaborate commentary.

---

[1] *Mémoire sur quelques Papyrus du Louvre*, Paris 1878.

EGYPTIAN TEXTS

This translation must necessarily be the basis of all others, but a modern treatment of the text is badly needed.

The text has been transcribed afresh and retranslated by one of us, and Professor Griffith was good enough to read through the pertinent passages of it with the translator, but owing to the difficulties both textual and otherwise with which it abounds, no consecutive translation would be intelligible without a bulky commentary which would be quite out of place in this book. We therefore decided merely to summarise the passages which directly concern us. The text abounds in mythological allusions which often render it extremely obscure. It must be confessed that there is little to be learned concerning mummification from the *Ritual of Embalming*, but it is of too great importance to be ignored.

§ i. Direction to the operator to anoint the mummy's head with frankincense. (*Pap. Boulaq*, 2, 1.)

§ ii. Direction to take an unguent vase filled with specified ointments such as are used for the *Opening of the Mouth*. An officiant called the " Treasurer of the God " is to anoint the whole body from the head to the soles of the feet, but omitting the head itself. (*Pap. Boulaq*, 2, 5–6.)

The " Treasurer of the God " appears to correspond to the ταριχευτης of the Greek texts.[1]

§ iii. The next direction is very obscure, and appears to refer to another anointing, and mentions the " children of Horus," which seem to refer to the

---

[1] The title, according to Blackman, is a legacy from the time when the burial ceremonies were performed for kings only. (See his article " Priest, Priesthood (Egyptian)," § XIV*d*, in *Hastings' Encyclopædia of Religion and Ethics*.)

separately embalmed viscera. (*Pap. Boulaq*, 2, 16–17.)

§ iv. Directions for the " children of Horus " and for anointing the back with " fat " (*mrḥ·t*). (*Pap. Boulaq*, 2, 18–20.)

§ v. Further directions for anointing and wrapping the back. Some reference is apparently made to filling the skull with medicaments. (*Pap. Boulaq*, 3, 13.)

§ vi. Directions for gilding the nails and winding the fingers in " linen of Sais." [1] (*Pap. Boulaq*, 3, 15.)

§ vii. Ceremonies performed by " Anubis, the chief of Mysteries," and " the Treasurer of the God." (*Pap. Boulaq*, 4, 7–8.)

Anubis was the embalmer, *par excellence*, and a priest impersonated him. This god is seen in innumerable tomb-pictures and papyri in attendance upon the mummy.

§ viii. A long section giving directions for the anointing and bandaging of the head, with a detailed specification of the bandages to be used for each part of the head, giving the magical names of each. Thus the descriptions and names of a long series of bandages are given for application to the ears, nostrils, cheeks, brow, occiput, mouth, chin, and neck. The application of these bandages is finished off by affixing a linen band of two fingers' width and anointing the whole

---

[1] The nails of mummies were often gilded in late times. (See Pettigrew : *Egyptian Mummies*, pp. 63–4.)
" Linen of Sais " is frequently mentioned in the texts, e.g. Stele of Amenhotpe, l. 12 (*Miss. Arch.*, vol. i, pp. 26 and 52), Loret : *Rec. de Travaux*, vol. iv, p. 22 ; Tomb of Khaemhēt (No. 57 = *Miss. Arch.*, vol. i, p. 130), etc.

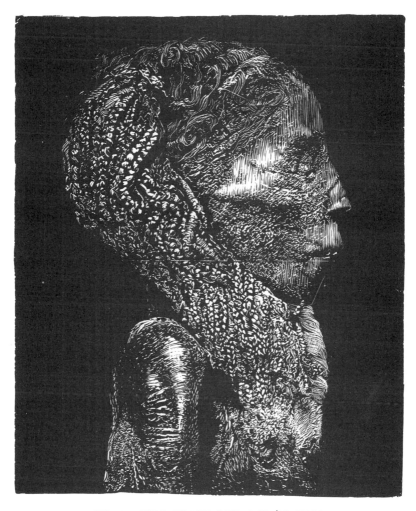

FIG. 9.——HEAD OF THE LADY RAY (PROFILE)

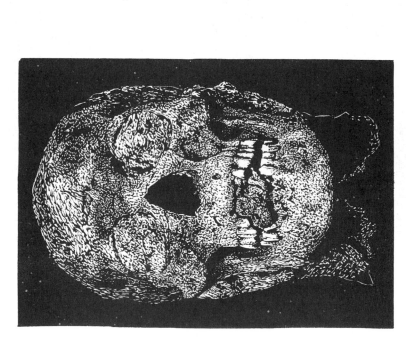

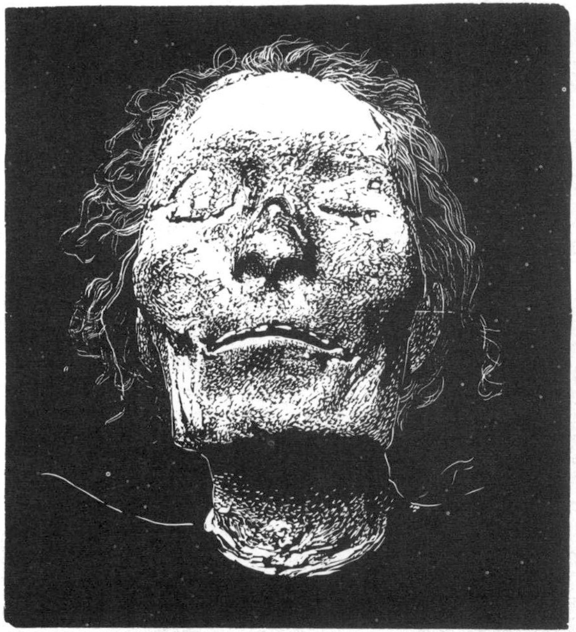

FIG. 11.—HEAD OF THE MUMMY OF AN UNKNOWN MAN.
(XVIIIth DYNASTY)

FIG. 10.—HEAD OF THE MUMMY OF THE FHARAOH
AMENOPHIS III. (XVIIIth DYNASTY)

FIG. 12.—MUMMY OF THE ELDER WOMAN FOUND IN THE TOMB OF AMENOPHIS II.
(XVIIIth DYNASTY)

FIG. 13.—MUMMY OF THE ELDER WOMAN FOUND IN THE TOMB OF AMENOPHIS II (PROFILE). (XVIIIth DYNASTY)

with " thick oil " (doubtless the resinous paste which is so often found upon actual mummies). (*Pap. Boulaq*, 4, 9–16.)

§ ix. Directions for further anointing of the head with frankincense and fat, and for enwrapping certain spices. (*Pap. Boulaq*, 7, 1–2.)

§ x. Long directions for anointing and wrapping of the hands. An ointment consisting of " Amu-flowers 1 part, Resin of Coptos 1, Natron 1." The bandages are all identified with gods and goddesses, and the vignette at the top of the papyrus shows several deities bringing bandages to the mummy lying on a couch. (*Pap. Boulaq*, 7, 7–16.)

§ xi. A similar passage describing bandages, with figures of gods, etc., traced upon them, used for the hands. (*Pap. Boulaq*, 8, 16–22.)

§ xii. Directions for the anointing and bandaging of the arms, feet and legs. (*Pap. Boulaq*, 9, 13–18 ; *Pap. Louvre*, 2, 1–7.)

These twelve directions, alternating with long incantations and prayers, are, as already mentioned, very elaborate but extremely obscure. It is difficult to believe that they were ever strictly carried out, but there is so little known as to the wrappings of actual mummies that it is unsafe to say whether inscribed bandages and other details of the ritual are verifiable or not. We know of no detailed account of the bandaging of late mummies, such as have been made in a few instances for earlier ones.[1] Possibly the burial with the mummy of a copy of the ritual was a sufficient substitute

---

[1] For the bandaging of two Middle-Kingdom mummies see M. A. Murray : *The Tomb of Two Brothers*, pp. 54–64 ; XVIIth Dynasty, Petrie : *Qurneh*, pp. 8, 9 ; XXIst Dynasty, Mace and Elliot Smith : *Annales du Service*, 1906, pp. 166–180 and Pls. IV–VI.

EGYPTIAN MUMMIES

for the actual performance of the details; but until an opportunity arises of examining the wrappings of a series of late mummies, judgment must be reserved. Various other points arising out of this text will be discussed after the next has been dealt with. This latter text is likewise found in two late funerary papyri—the Bilingual Rhind Papyri at Edinburgh.

2. *The Rhind Papyri.*—These two papyri were found by A. H. Rhind in an XVIIIth Dynasty tomb at Thebes, which was occupied by an intrusive burial of several mummies of the Ptolemaic Period. An account of the discovery of the tomb was given shortly after by Rhind in his book on the Theban Tombs [1] and a coloured facsimile by Netherclift, with a translation and notes by Dr. Birch, followed shortly after.[2] The text, which is written both in hieratic and demotic characters, was exhaustively studied by Brugsch, who devoted a special memoir to it.[3] With the great development of demotic scholarship in recent years a new edition of the text was needed, and this was undertaken by the late Dr. Möller, who published an admirable edition of the papyri, with transcriptions, translations and an elaborate and valuable commentary.[4]

The composition [5] of the papyri is akin to the various late funerary works, such as the *Book of Breathings, May my Name Flourish*, etc. A certain section, however, affects embalming, and the rendering given below is based upon that of Möller. This section immediately follows the reception of the deceased by Anubis.

---

[1] *Thebes, its Tombs and their Tenants*, pp. 77 ff. (1862).
[2] *Facsimiles of Two Papyri found in a Tomb at Thebes*, 1863.
[3] *A. H. Rhind's Zwei Bilingue Papyri*, Leipzig 1865.
[4] *Die Beiden Totenpapyrus Rhind*, Leipzig, 1913.
[5] Möller: *op. cit.* § iv, pp. 8 and 10, where the contents of the text are given in tabular form.

EGYPTIAN TEXTS

Thou camest joyfully out of the operating-chamber. To thee were eight processions (ceremonies) made, divided into thirty-six days. Thou camest forth, I made for thee the ceremony of the Great Lake of Khons, rest (?) in the tomb-chamber of the necropolis of thy town. (There were made ?) nine ceremonies until the seventieth day, because of the seventeen members of the god as follows :—

> The seven openings of the head,
> The four sons of Horus,
> The two legs,
> The two arms,
> The breast,
> The back,   Total 17,

divided into seventy days in the embalming-room. The Great Isis, the mother of the god, commands to make the beautiful burial of N.[1] Two hundred and six *hin* of fat were boiled as is done for a sacred animal. Thou wast rubbed with balsam by Horus, the lord of the laboratory. Shesmu wound with his fingers the divine bandage in order to enwrap thy body with the wrappings of the gods and goddesses. Anubis as embalmer filled thy skull with resin, corn of the gods, . . . cedar oil, mild ox-fat, cinnamon oil; and myrrh is to all thy members. Thy body was invested with holy bandages. Come forth to see the winter sun on the 26th day of Pharmuthi.[2]

The other papyrus has a somewhat similar passage :—

Isis went to the burial of N. Fat was boiled for her as is done for the mother of a sacred animal. For her balsam was rubbed in by Horus, lord of the laboratory. Shesmu wound with his fingers the divine bandage, in order to wrap up thy body with the bandages of the gods and goddesses. Anubis the embalmer furnishes thy body with ointment and bandages. Thou comest forth because thou art provided with thine adornment in the likeness of Hathor, mistress of the western land, and seest the winter sun in his sacred boat on the 26th day of Choiakh.[3]

Combining the material of these two texts the passage may be paraphrased as follows :—

---

[1] Here follow the name, titles and filiation of the deceased.
[2] Pap. Rhind No. 1, p. 3, 1 ff. (hieratic text). The corresponding demotic text is substantially the same. Möller : *op. cit.* pp. 18 ff.
[3] Pap. Rhind, No. 2, p. 4, l. 1 ff. (hieratic text). Möller : *op. cit.* p. 58.

EGYPTIAN MUMMIES

The deceased (in the first text a man, in the second a woman) is taken triumphantly from the operating-room,[1] and eight ceremonies are then performed over a period of thirty-six days. The corpse is then laid in a chamber of the necropolis, where nine further ceremonies are enacted until the 70th day, in honour of the seventeen members of the god (Osiris). These are detailed and may be summarised thus :—

(i)	The seven openings of the head ..	7
(ii)	The four children of Horus	4
(iii)	The two legs	2
(iv)	The two arms	2
(v)	The breast	1
(vi)	The back	1
	Total	17

This total of seventeen equals the eight ceremonies up to the 36th day and nine up to the 70th day mentioned above. Isis then orders the burial. Two hundred and six measures (*hin*) of fat are boiled for the embalming, as is done for the embalming of the sacred animals,[2] and a mortuary priest, impersonating Horus, rubs the body over with balsam. Another priest (Shesmu) winds the bandages to complete investiture of the deceased in the bandages of the gods and goddesses. The embalmer, impersonating Anubis, fills the skull with medicaments and a further wrapping in bandages ensues. The corpse is then ready for his introduction to the next world, which is here expressed as meeting the winter sun.

---

[1] Where the flank incision was made and the viscera and brain excised.
[2] See the study of the Apis bull's embalming in Spiegelberg, *Aegyptische Zeitschrift*, t. 56, pp. 1 ff. (1920).

EGYPTIAN TEXTS

In the ceremonies i–vi above, there is no evidence whatever on which to suppose, as Brugsch [1] and Revillout [2] have done, that "openings" are to be understood in the case of Nos. ii–vi. The text specifies seventeen ceremonies to be performed upon seventeen named parts of the body, the first seven of which are the natural openings of the head, viz. the eyes, ears, nostrils and mouth. The Egyptian word here used is *ro*, which means literally a mouth. In the other cases a different word is used, which, although connected with the verbal root "open," means a procession or ceremony, and the attempt to reconcile the artificial openings made in the body for the purpose of "packing" it with the statement in the text, is therefore based on faulty premises. [3]

We can perhaps trace a relationship between this text and the Ritual of Embalming. The four children of Horus (i.e. the viscera) are dealt with in § iii and § iv of the Ritual; [4] the legs and arms in § xii, and the back in § iv. Directions are given in § viii for various parts of the head, including the ears, nostrils and mouth, and the filling of the skull, rendered empty by the removal of the brain, has its echo in § v of the Ritual. The "bandages of the gods and goddesses" are likewise detailed in §§ viii, x and xi.

The next texts to mention, like the last, state the period occupied by the embalming and subsequent ceremonies.

3. *The Stele of Dhout.*—The inscription relating to the funeral ceremonies has been published by Gardiner, [5] and the part which now concerns us he renders as follows :—

A goodly burial arrives in peace, thy seventy days having been fulfilled in thy place of embalming.

---

[1] *Op. cit. supra.*
[2] *Aegyptische Zeitschrift*, t. 18, p. 102.
[3] Elliot Smith : *Mémoires de l'Inst. Eg.*, t. v, pp. 43 ff. (1906).
[4] See above, pp. 47–8.
[5] *The Tomb of Amenemhēt*, p. 56

EGYPTIAN MUMMIES

This stele is in Theban Tomb No. 110, and dates from the reign of Queen Hatshepsowet. The same text occurs in the Theban Tomb of Antef (No. 164), which is of the reign of Tuthmosis III.

4. *British Museum Stele No.* 378.[1]—This stele, which belongs to a priest of Ptolemaic date, states that he had " a goodly burial after the seventy days of his embalming had been fulfilled."

5. *Story of Satne Khamuas.*—In this demotic story a passage occurs in which the period of embalming is mentioned.[2] It is rendered by Griffith as follows :—

And Pharaoh caused to be given to him entry into the Good House [3] of (?) sixteen days, wrapping up of (?) thirty-five days, coffining in seventy days and he was laid to rest in his sarcophagus in his house of rest.

6. *Inscription of Anemher.*—A text which is published in Brugsch : *Thesaurus,* p. 893, is translated by Griffith,[4] which gives particulars as to time, and in this case a period of seventy days is again stated, the burial taking place on the seventy-first day. The following is Griffith's rendering:—

They made for him a burying from the 28th Pharmuti, which was his 4th day (he died on the 24th) according to that that comes in writing, unto the 9th Epiphi, his 71st day making for him every necessary and suitable thing that is customary therein according to that that comes in writing. The 20th Payni to the 29th (?) they cooked unguents, they bound on him the bandages and clothes of byssus and the amulets that are proper for the nobles of Egypt. They made for him every purification, every cleansing (?) ; they made for him a great and fine coffin according to that that comes in writing from the sixth Epiphi to the end of the mourning, he having entered his house of rest in which his father lay.

---

[1] Sharpe : *Egyptian Inscriptions,* vol. i, Pl. XLVIII. Budge : *Guide to Egyptian Galleries (Sculpture), Brit. Mus.,* p. 266 (1909).
[2] Griffith : *Stories of the High Priests of Memphis,* p. 29.
[3] " The Good House " or " Beautiful House " is a frequent appellation for the embalmers' workshop. See Gardiner : *Tomb of Amenemhēt,* p. 72.
[4] *Op. cit.* pp. 29, 30.

EGYPTIAN TEXTS

From this it follows that the embalming was carried on up to the 52nd day, the wrapping up to the 67th day, the coffining from the 68th to the 70th day, and the burial on the 71st.[1]

The frequent repetition of the period of 70 days, the fixed order of procedure, and the reference to " that that comes in writing," makes it evident that the rites of embalming were carried out in conformity with a definite canon, which, however, has not survived.

7. *Bologna Stele No.* 1042.—A hand copy of this stele is given by Piehl in his *Inscriptions hiéroglyphiques*, t. i, Pl. XXXVI (text, part i, p. 43). It reads as follows :—

Year 22. Payni 24th day. On this day was buried the Osiris N,[2] after 80 days of embalming. He was happily buried by his eldest son, the prophet Her-ab.

This mention of eighty days is quite exceptional, although, if Piehl's copy is to be trusted, there is no doubt about the reading.

8. *Florence Ostracon No.* 2616.[3] This ostracon contains a fragment of a literary work in which is an allusion to the four canopic jars. The speaker states that the King

gave me my four jars for my mummy and my sarcophagus of alabaster.

The following references are given for the sake of completeness, and refer to the materials used in mummification.

9. *Papyrus Leiden No.*344.—This papyrus, which contains a long series of admonitions of an Egyptian sage upon the disastrous condition into which Egypt had sunk during his time, refers to the importance of cedar oil for mummification.[4]

---

[1] In the same note Griffith cites three other references to Brugsch (*Thesaurus*) which concern priests.
[2] Here follows the name of the deceased with a long list of priestly titles.
[3] Golenischeff : *Rec. de Trav.*, vol. iii, 3 ff.
[4] Gardiner : *The Admonitions of an Egyptian Sage*, p. 32.

55

EGYPTIAN MUMMIES

Men do not sail northwards to [Byblos] to-day. What shall we do for cedars for our mummies with the produce of which priests are buried, and with the oil of which [chiefs] are embalmed. . . .

10. *Theban Tombs of Senufer and Amenemhab.*—There is a scene in each of these tombs in which the deceased is seen inspecting the burial outfit given to him by the King and in the relative inscription this phrase occurs :—

Fat for embalming the mummy.[1]

Before passing on to the Greek texts (Chapter **IV**), reference may be made to an interesting demotic letter in the British Museum. This papyrus (No. 10,077), which is dated in the 16th year of Ptolemy Philadelphus, is an undertaking by an embalmer to mummify the body of his client's son. The client provides the natron, bandages and other necessaries, and the embalmer engages to prepare the body in the prescribed manner in seventy-two days and to hand it over duly treated. In default he promises to pay a fine. A photograph of the papyrus, together with a translation and commentary of the text, has been published by Spiegelberg.[2]

It will be noticed that the period is here stated to be seventy-two days, but perhaps the actual embalming occupied seventy days, the other two days being for transit to and from the embalmers' premises.

---

[1] Sethe : *Urkunden*, iv, pp. 538 and 913.
[2] *Zeitschrift für äg. Sprache*, vol. 54 (1918), pp. 111–114 and Pl. IV.

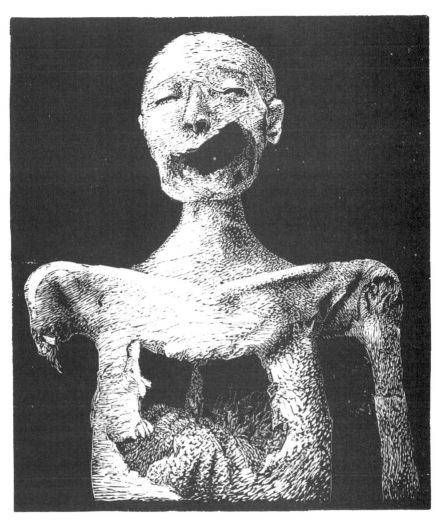

FIG. 14.—MUMMY OF THE YOUNGER WOMAN FOUND IN THE TOMB OF
AMENOPHIS II

Showing the damage done by plunderers to the face and chest.

(XVIIIth Dynasty)

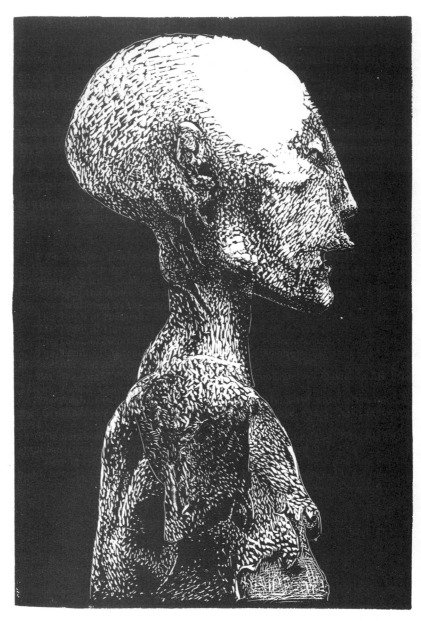

FIG. 15.—THE YOUNGER WOMAN FROM THE TOMB OF AMENOPHIS II
(PROFILE). (XVIIIth DYNASTY)

FIG. 16.—MUMMY OF THE YOUNG PRINCE FOUND IN THE TOMB OF AMENOPHIS II, SHOWING THE " HORUS-LOCK."

The large hole in the chest is the work of ancient plunderers.   (XVIIIth Dynasty)

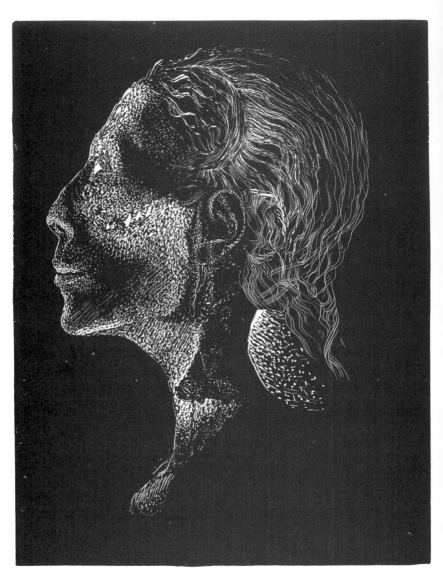

FIG. 17.—HEAD OF THE MUMMY OF THE PHARAOH TUTHMOSIS IV.
(XVIIIth DYNASTY)

CHAPTER IV

EMBALMING ACCORDING TO HERODOTUS
AND LATER AUTHORS

A S the Egyptians themselves have left us little or no literature on the technical processes of mummification, we have to rely very largely upon the testimony of later writers, principally of Herodotus (fifth century B.C.), and of Diodorus Siculus (about 400 years later). As the statements of these two writers contain much information which is of great importance, intermingled with less reliable matter, it will be worth while to quote their statements in full with some comments thereon.

The account of Herodotus is as follows :— [1]

Their (*sc.* the Egyptians') manner of mourning and of burial is as follows : When any person of distinction in a family dies, all the women of the household besmear their heads and even their faces with mud, and, leaving the corpse in the house, they wander about the town beating themselves, with clothes girt up and their breasts bare, all their relatives accompanying them. The men, too, beat themselves, their clothes being girt up likewise. After having done thus, they escort the corpse to its embalming. There are certain persons who carry on that craft (i.e. embalming) and who are skilled in their art ; these persons, when the corpse is brought to them, show to the bearers wooden models of corpses painted in imitation of the originals. They show that which they describe as the most perfect manner of embalming, whose name I hold it to be improper to mention in such a connexion. They then show the second,

[1] Book II, §§ 85–88. The Greek text of Dietsch (Leipzig, Teubner, 1885) has been used. We are indebted to Mr. E. E. Trotman for a revision of this translation as well as of our translation of Diodorus and for many valuable suggestions thereon.

which is inferior and less expensive, and then the third, which is the cheapest. And having explained them all, they enquire from them in what style they desire to have the corpse prepared, and having agreed upon the cost, the relatives straightway depart ; but the embalmers, remaining in their workshop, thus proceed to embalm in the most costly manner.

First they draw out the brain through the nostrils with an iron hook, taking part of it out in this way, the rest by pouring in drugs. Next, with a sharp Ethiopian stone they make an incision in the flank, and take out all the entrails, and after cleansing the body and scouring it with palm-wine, they purify it with pounded incense ; then, having filled the body with pure pounded myrrh and cassia and other perfumes, frankincense excepted, they sew it up again. Having done thus they soak the body in natron, keeping it covered for seventy days, for it is not lawful to soak it for a longer time than this. And when the seventy days are accomplished, they wash the corpse, and wrap the whole body in fine linen cut into strips, smearing it with gum, which the Egyptians use instead of glue. After this the relatives, having taken the corpse back again, make a wooden case of human shape, and having made it, place the corpse inside, and having closed it up, put it in a sepulchral chamber, standing it upright against the wall. It is thus that the most expensive manner of embalming the dead is performed.

For those who desire the medium style to avoid heavy expense, they prepare the corpse thus : Having charged their syringes with cedar oil, they fill the inside of the corpse, without making any incision or removing the viscera, but inject it at the anus. Then they close the aperture to prevent the liquid from escaping and soak the body in natron for the prescribed number of days. On the last day they let out the cedar oil which had been previously injected, and, such is its potency that it brings away the bowels and internal parts in a fluid state, and the natron dissolves the flesh so that nothing remains but skin and bones. When this has been done they return the body without further manipulation.

The third manner of embalming is this, which is used only for persons of slender means. After washing out the body with a purgative they soak it in natron for seventy days and deliver it to be taken back.[1]

In order to estimate the value of Herodotus' account, it must first be remembered that he visited Egypt at a time when Greek influence was becoming stronger and stronger, and was gradually superseding customs which had held

---

[1] § 89, not translated here, is discussed in Chapter VIII in connexion with certain Ptolemaic practices in Nubia. (See p. 126.)

full sway in Egypt for many centuries before. It must also be remembered that the embalmer's art was a sacred and religious function, of which he could scarcely have been an eye-witness and upon which his information must have come at second-hand. On the whole, however, his account is borne out fairly well by an examination of actual mummies belonging to earlier periods, for in late mummies bitumen applied hot was commonly used, the action of which renders examination of the body very difficult. It is certain, moreover, that more than three methods of embalming were used, as great variation occurs in the treatment of individual mummies, as will be seen hereafter. Nor was it until quite late times that mummification passed into general use for persons other than the wealthy and priestly classes.

The opening statements of Herodotus as to mourning are confirmed by numerous pictures of funeral processions which abound in tombs of all periods and in countless papyri, and the mourning doubtless began immediately death took place, as the death scene in a tomb at Saqqara testifies.[1] The female mourners at funeral processions are generally represented with bare breasts and dishevelled hair, and the usual attitude of their hands suggests that their action is that of putting mud or dust upon their heads, a practice which is common in Egypt at the present day. In one instance at least the female mourners have their clothes " girt up " to the pitch of indecency.[2]

The transport of the corpse to the embalmers' workshop was doubtless carried out with due ceremony, for in an Old Kingdom tomb, that of Pepionkh at Meir, Herodotus' very

---

[1] Bissing : *Denkmäler Aeg. Sculptur*, Pl. XVIIIв = Capart : *Rue de Tombeaux*, Pl. LXXI.
[2] Theban Tomb of Neferhotpe (No. 49). The scene is reproduced in Maspero : *Struggle of the Nations*, p. 515.

words are foreshadowed in the legend to the picture: " escourting to the workshop of the embalmer." [1]

The models of mummies in their miniature coffins must have been familiar objects in Egypt, and doubtless gave rise to Herodotus' statement that they were kept as models by the embalmers, although the actual purpose of their employment was very different.[2]

The employment of special persons for the embalmer's art is quite borne out by the facts. In Pharaonic times the embalmer was called the *wt* and impersonated Anubis. Blackman has suggested [3] that the embalmers, even in ancient times, appear to have belonged to a gild or organisation of their own, a fact which we know to have been the case in the Græco-Roman period.

In this latter period the embalmers were of two kinds, the incision-makers or παρασχισταί, and the embalmers and wrappers (ταριχευταί). In the *Ritual of Embalming* (*supra*, p. 47) and other texts various other ministrants are named: *lectors, sem-priests, imy-khant priests,* and the " *Treasurers of the God.*" [4]

Herodotus scrupulously abstains from naming the first method of embalming. The missing name is evidently Osiris.

On the question of price we will defer our remarks until we deal with the account of Diodorus, who is more specific in this detail.

The removal of the brain through the nostrils is confirmed by innumerable mummies, which will be hereafter described, and which often have fragments of brain-matter left behind

---

[1] This tomb, copied by Dr. Blackman, is not yet published, but the above phrase is quoted by Gardiner: *Tomb of Amenemhēt*, p. 45, note 4.

[2] For such model mummies and coffins see, for example, Quibell: *Tomb of Yuaa and Thuiu*, Pl. XIX.

[3] Article "Priest, Priesthood (Egyptian)," § xiv, b (i), in *Hastings' Encyclopædia of Religion and Ethics.*   [4] See *supra*, p. 47

in the skull, which the embalmers did not always succeed in removing by the very difficult method of groping with a hook through the fractured ethmoid bone, which had to be perforated in order to reach the interior of the head. The flank incision also is too well known to need more than a passing reference, but it is rare to find it sewn up,[1] the general custom being to leave it gaping open, later to be covered by a metal or wax plate.

It is curious to note that the body-cavity was packed with aromatic substances *before* its immersion in the salt-bath. Herodotus is evidently at fault here, as not only probability, but the evidence of the mummies themselves, is against this.[2] Again, he states that the body is kept immersed for seventy days, but in this he is contradicted by the Egyptian evidence detailed in the previous chapter, from which the fact emerges that the whole process of embalming occupied seventy days, only one half of this period being devoted to the soaking process. The statement is noteworthy that it was unlawful to occupy more than seventy days, this again being evidence that the embalming process was carried out in strict accordance with a definite canon, which is implied by text No. 6, translated in the previous chapter.

The wrapping of the mummy, as the Egyptian texts show, was a long and complicated process, but its significance was evidently not grasped by Herodotus, who refers to it very cursorily in connexion with the first method of embalming and does not mention it at all in connexion with the other two methods ; but one important feature, the use of gum,[3] has not escaped him.

---

[1] See below, p. 119.

[2] Lucas holds that in some cases at least the treatment of the body-cavity was carried out prior to immersion. *Journ. Egypt. Arch.*, t. 1, p. 119

[3] I.e. resinous paste.

EGYPTIAN MUMMIES

The practice of standing the mummy upright and of keeping it above ground was not customary until late times, when, as Petrie has clearly shown from the mummies of the Roman period found by him at Hawara, they were kept for long periods before burial. In earlier times it was customary to place the mummy upright only for the performance of the final ceremonies before its interment.[1]

The second method of embalming emphasises the use of cedar oil, which was at all times an important factor in mummification; [2] but although mummies without incisions and retaining their internal organs are known,[3] we have no Egyptian evidence of the use of syringes. There is no doubt that mummies were sometimes treated in this manner, and therefore some mechanical means must have been employed to inject the oil, which could only thus have been forced through the convolutions of the intestines. (See p. 79.)

The third method apparently aims at nothing more than washing out the body, and then salting it.

In all cases the salt-bath is used and for the same period.

We will now give the account of Diodorus Siculus :

When a person amongst them dies, all his relatives and friends, putting mud upon their heads, go about the town lamenting, until the time of burying the body. In the meantime they abstain from bathing and from wine and all kinds of delicacies, neither do they wear fine apparel. They have three manners of burial : one very costly, one medium and one modest. Upon the first a talent of silver is spent, upon the second

---

[1] Petrie : *Hawara*, p. 15. For the rites before the mummy see above, p. 41. In the Theban Tomb of Haremhab (No. 78) the unusual scene occurs of two mummies, standing upright upon a sledge, being drawn towards an open shrine which awaits them with open doors. Bouriant : *Le Tombeau de Harmhabi (Mem. Miss. Arch.,* t. v, Pl. VI).

[2] See the Leyden papyrus quoted above, p. 55.

[3] E.g. the interesting series of XIth Dynasty princesses found under the temple of Mentuhotpe at Deir-el-Bahari by the excavators of the Metropolitan Museum of New York, and also various others referred to in succeeding chapters.

twenty minæ, but in the third there is very little cost. Those who attend to the bodies have learned their art from their forefathers. These, carrying to the household of the deceased illustrations of the costs of burial of each kind, ask them in which manner they desire the body to be treated. When all is agreed upon, and the corpse is handed over, they (*sc.* the relatives) deliver the body to those who are appointed to deal with it in the accustomed manner.

First, he who is called the scribe,[1] laying the body down, marks on the left flank where it is to be cut. Then he who is called the cutter [2] takes an Ethiopian stone, and cuts the flesh as the law prescribes, and forthwith escapes running, those who are present pursuing and throwing stones and cursing, as though turning the defilement [of his act] on to *his* head. For whosoever inflicts violence upon, or wounds, or in any way injures a body of his own kind, they hold worthy of hatred. The embalmers,[3] on the other hand, they esteem worthy of every honour and respect, associating with the priests and being admitted to the temples without hindrance as holy men. When they have assembled for the treatment of the body which has been cut, one of them inserts his hand through the wound in the corpse into the breast and takes out everything *excepting the kidneys and the heart.* Another man cleanses each of the entrails, sweetening them with palm-wine and with incense. Finally, having washed the whole body, they first diligently treat it with cedar oil and other things for over thirty days, and then with myrrh and cinnamon and [spices], which not only have the power to preserve it for a long time, but also impart a fragrant smell. Having treated it, they restore it to the relatives with every member of the body preserved so perfectly that even the eyelashes and eyebrows remain, the whole appearance of the body being unchangeable, and the cast of the features recognisable. Therefore, many of the Egyptians, keeping the bodies of their ancestors in fine chambers, can behold at a glance those who died before they themselves were born. Thus, while they contemplate the size and proportions of their bodies, and even the very lineaments of their faces, they present an example of a kind of inverted necromancy and seem to live in the same age with those upon whom they look.

Diodorus gives several particulars which are not mentioned by Herodotus, and as he lived four hundred years later than the latter, mummification had deteriorated still further from its ancient standards in his time.

On the manner of mourning both authors agree, but Diodorus adds that it was kept up until the time of burial,

---

[1] καὶ πρῶτος μὲν ὁ γραμματεὺς λεγόμενος.
[2] ἔπειθ' ὁ λεγόμενος παρασχίστης. [3] οἱ ταριχευταί.

EGYPTIAN MUMMIES

and that washing and luxuries were forgone by the mourners. Although three modes of burial are again specified, only one of them, the costliest, is described. The mention of specific prices, and the reference to the written statement of them, seems to imply that a fixed tariff of charges was in use in Diodorus' time, but all the evidence we have as to the cost of embalming, in a few Greek papyri, does not lend probability to his statement.

The first of these papyri reads as follows :— [1]

ACCOUNT OF FUNERAL EXPENSES.

. . . .	12 dr.	2 ob.
Earthenware pot		2 ob.
Red paint	4 dr.	19 ob.
Wax..	12 dr.	
Myrrh	4 dr.	4 ob.
Song (? dirge)		4 ob.
Tallow		8 ob.
Linen clothes	136 dr.	16 ob.
Mask	64 dr.	
Cedar oil	41 dr.	
Medicament for the linen cloth	4 dr.	
Good oil	4 dr.	
Turbon's wages	8 dr.	
Lamp-wicks	24 dr.	
Cost of an old tunic		24 ob.
Sweet wine..		20 ob.
Barley	16 dr.	
Leaven	4 dr.	
Dog	8 dr.	
Little mask (?)	14 dr.	
2 artabæ of loaves	21 dr.	
Pine cone (?)		8 ob.
Mourners	32 dr.	
Carriage by donkey	8 dr.	
Chaff (??)		12 ob.
Total	440 dr.	16 ob.

[1] Mr. H. I. Bell kindly referred us to this interesting document and supplied us with the above translation (from which we have omitted the philological notes and the translation of the last lines, which relate to another subject).

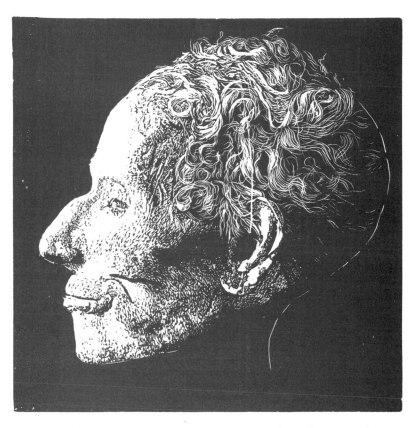

FIG. 18.—HEAD OF THE MUMMY OF YUAA (XVIIIth DYNASTY)

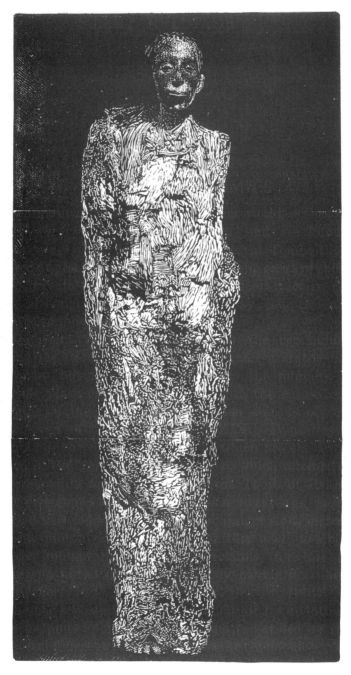

FIG. 19.—MUMMY OF THUIU, WIFE OF YUAA. (XVIIIth DYNASTY)

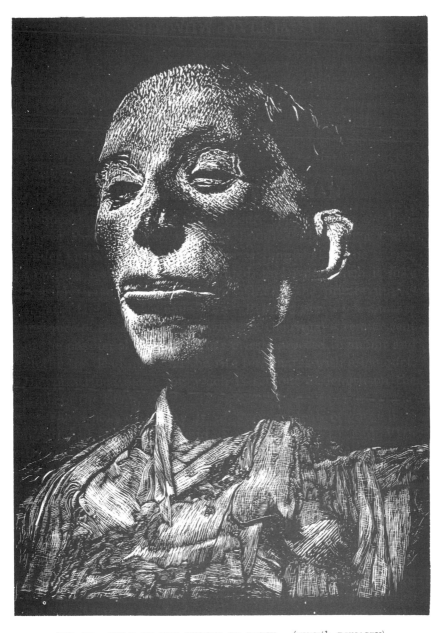

FIG. 20.—HEAD OF THE MUMMY OF THUIU (XVIIIth DYNASTY)

FIG. 21 —HEAD OF THE PHARAOH SETY I,
(xixth DYNASTY)

HERODOTUS AND LATER AUTHORS

In this important and interesting document, which dates from the second or third century A.D., it will be observed that many of the substances named by Herodotus and Diodorus occur. The large quantity of linen used is shown by the high cost of that item. The mask was also costly. A few of the items are obscure, but the " dog " may possibly be a figure of Anubis, who is often called the dog in Greek texts.

Another papyrus of the same nature, and dating from the end of the first century A.D., has been published by Grenfell and Hunt in the *Amherst Papyri*, p. 150, No. 125.[1]

Account for the expenses of a mummy. My expenses : Cedar oil, 4 drachmæ ; 2 cotylæ of olive-oil, 20 obols ; an earthenware pot, 1 ob ; for a mask and . . ., 24 dr. ; to the mummifier, 11 dr. ; for a necklace (?) of 4 minæ weight, 810 ob. Expenses of Thermouthis (?) and Harpagathos : Linen cloth and Harpagathos' tunic, . . . [dr.] ; another tunic for Thermouthis' son . . . [dr.] ; oil . . . [dr.] ; to the mummifier . . . [The rest is lost.]

We may quote one more document in this connexion of the third century A.D., which is less detailed and is more fragmentary in condition :—

Account for expenses for the corpse : The expenses were for the burial . . . at 48 drachmæ ; wages of the bearers . . ., 16 dr. 20 ob. ; wreaths, 12 ob. ; a . . . of wine . . ., 4 dr. 20 ob.[2]

Diodorus states that the embalmers' office is hereditary, a statement which is confirmed by a group of demotic papyri published by Revillout.[3]

The text is published in Wesseley : *Studien für Paläographie und Papyrologie*, vol. xxii, No. 56. Cf. Wilcken : *Archiv. für Pap.*, t. vii, p. 107 (1923).

[1] We again acknowledge our indebtedness to Mr. H. I. Bell for referring us to Wilcken's *Grundzüge und Chrestomathie der Papyruskunde*, where we found references to the above and some of the other Greek papyri quoted in this chapter.

[2] Grenfell and Hunt : *Fayûm Towns and their Papyri*, p. 250, No. 103.

[3] " Une Famille de Paraschistes ou Taricheutes thébains," in the *Aegyptische Zeitschrift*, t. xvii (1879), pp. 83–92.

EGYPTIAN MUMMIES

An interesting detail which is lacking in Herodotus' account, is supplied by Diodorus, who states that a scribe (doubtless the *lector* of Pharaonic times) traces a line for the flank incision, and that the cutter, having performed his task, flies from the curses and missiles of those who witnessed it. Up to the present the statement is unconfirmed, and it is idle to comment upon it.

Both writers agree that the incision is made with an Ethiopian stone, but no reason for the use of this implement is given at a time when metal tools had been in common use for many centuries. Both agree in the statement that the viscera were removed, but Diodorus significantly adds " *except the kidneys and the heart.*"

The importance of this will be discussed in a later chapter when the special treatment of the viscera is dealt with (see below, p. 145). In this connexion, although neither Herodotus nor Diodorus informs us what happened to the organs after they had been removed and cleansed, two other classical writers refer to them, namely Porphyry and Plutarch.

The passage from Porphyry is as follows :— [1]

" There is one point which must not be passed over, namely, that when they embalm the dead of the wealthy class, among other observances paid to the corpse, they privately remove the intestines and place them in a chest, which they make fast and present before the Sun, while one of those occupied in embalming the body recites a prayer. And this prayer, which Ekphantos translated from his native language, is to the following effect : ' O Lord Sun and all you gods who give life to men, receive me favourably and commit me to abide with the everlasting gods. For as long as I continued in that life, I have steadfastly reverenced

---

[1] *De Abstinentia*, iv, 10. For this and the following translations from Plutarch, we are indebted to Mr. E. E. Trotman.

the gods whom my parents instructed me to worship, and I have ever honoured those who brought my body into the world ; while, as concerns my fellow-men, I have done no murder, nor betrayed a trust, nor committed any other deadly sin. But if, during my life, I have sinned in eating or drinking what was unlawful, the fault was not mine, but of this ' (showing the chest in which was the stomach)."

It is interesting to note that, according to this author, the internal parts are regarded as the seat of evil emotions, just as the heart and kidneys (as we shall presently see), which were *not* excised from the body, were looked upon as the seat of the mind and of good emotions. The prayer which is recited during the exposure of the chest to the Sun is in many ways reminiscent of the texts on countless Egyptian stelæ, wherein the deceased parades his good actions, and the latter part recalls the so-called " Negative Confession " in § 125 of the *Book of the Dead.*

Plutarch has two references to the viscera, which are of similar purport :—

Who, cutting open the corpse, displayed it to the Sun, and then cast those parts (the intestines) into the river, and turned their attention to the rest of the body, which had now become purified.[1]

and again :—

In the case of the well-to-do, they imitate the Egyptians, who open their dead and extract the intestines, which they cast out before the Sun as chargeable with all the sins the man has committed.[2]

The destruction of any part of the body was dreaded by the Pharaonic Egyptians, and the *Book of the Dead* and other texts are full of prayers that the body shall be complete and that no part of it shall be taken away, although it is a curious

---

[1] Plutarch VII, *Sap. Conv.,* XVI. Ed. Didot, p. 188.
[2] *De Carnium Esu, Oratio Posterior.* Ed. Didot, p. 1219.

fact that we have no record, either Egyptian or Greek, of the fate of the brain after it had been removed, nor has any mummy yet been found in which the brain or any part of it, once removed, has been preserved along with the viscera.

Diodorus makes no reference at all to the salt-bath, but he states that the washing and anointing takes more than thirty days to perform, a period which is in accordance with the Egyptian texts already cited (*supra*, pp. 53–56). He not only ignores the bandaging, but by his statements as to the recognition of the features of the dead, even ancestors who had long been dead, it is implied that no bandaging was applied, a fact which is quite contrary to the evidence of contemporary mummies. Possibly, however, the allusion is to the painted portrait panels used in late times.

Mummies of the Græco-Roman period are often found with labels bearing their names attached to them.[1] These labels were tied to the neck and were for identification when mummies were buried in pits or caves and piled one on another. They were also used when a body was sent for embalming or burial by carrier, as the following Greek papyrus shows :—[2]

> Senpamonthes to Pamonthes her brother, greeting. I am sending you the body of my mother, Senuris, having a label[3] on its neck, by Tales, father of Hierax, in a boat suitable (for this purpose), the cost having been completely defrayed by me. This is a description of the body. It has on the outside a rose-coloured shroud and the name is written upon the region of the belly. I pray for your lasting health.

One of the Oxyrhynchus Papyri refers to the transport of a mummy, which was not ready for despatch when the messengers arrived for it.[4]

---

[1] E.g. Petrie : *Dendereh*, p. 32. On the subject of mummy labels see the important article by Krebs : *Aeg. Zeit.*, 32 (1894), pp. 36–51.

[2] The text of this papyrus (second or third century A.D.) and an account of its contents, not a full translation, is given by Wilcken, *op. cit.*, t. ii, No. 499. Text No. 498 is similar. [3] ταβλα.

[4] A. S. Hunt : *Oxyrhynchus Papyri*, pt. vii, No. 1068, pp. 223, 224.

HERODOTUS AND LATER AUTHORS

Yet another text, the label attached to a case containing three bodies, relating to the transport and burial of mummies in Greek times, must be quoted, as it gives directions for the burial of the bodies in the Theban necropolis.[1]

> For the Tomb of Seneponyx. My daughter, Ptahmonthē, daughter of Papsenis, and his own daughter are packed herein. I have completely defrayed the cost of transport and all other charges. Will you place it (*sc.* the case) within the tombs which are in the Memnonia?

A Greek papyrus in the Louvre[2] is a letter to the governor of the district, notifying the violation of a tomb. After the customary salutations it proceeds :—

> In the year XLIV, while Lochus my parent had gone to Diospolis, certain persons entered one of the tombs which belong to me in the Thebaid, and having opened it, despoiled some of the mummies buried there and at the same time carried off all the gear which I had deposited there, amounting to the value of 10 talents of copper. In consequence, as the door was left wide open, the well-preserved bodies had suffered from wolves, which had partly devoured them.

The termination of the letter is a request that the guilty parties should be found and brought to justice.

Mummification persisted in Egypt long after its purpose was not only nullified but reversed by the introduction of Christianity. Very many mummies of the Coptic period are known which are debased but undoubted examples of the embalmer's art. Coptic literature is silent on the subject of embalming,[3] but we have contemporary and mediæval

---

[1] Revillout : *Aegyptische Zeitschrift*, t. xviii (1880), p. 107. A very large number of Greek mummy labels will be found translated by Krebs in the article previously cited.

[2] Papyrus No. 6, published in *Notices et Extraits des Manuscrits*, t. xviii, pt. ii, pp. 160 ff. (1858).

[3] We owe this information to Mr. W. E. Crum, to whom we are also indebted for many valuable references to Coptic burial customs, among which the most important is to the article of Carl Schmidt in the *Aegyptische Zeitschrift*, t. xxxii (1894), pp. 52 ff.

references to it in Greek and Latin texts, where the fathers of the Church inveigh against it as a pagan custom and inconsistent with Christian beliefs. The early Christians often embalmed the bodies of martyrs and holy men out of reverence and respect for them.

The embalming of the martyrs in Egypt is referred to in the following passage of the Syriac text of the *Paradise of the Fathers*. After their martyrdom, the holy Apollo and his companions were visited by their followers :—·

> And we ourselves saw the martyrium wherein he and those who had testified with him were laid, and we prayed and worshipped God, and also touched their dead bodies, for they were not as yet buried because of the inundation of the Nile, but lay embalmed upon their biers in Thebaïs, and for this reason we made ready to insert here the history of the man.[1]

In the Syriac version of the life of St. Anthony, by Athanasius, the saint addresses his faithful brethren as he feels his end approaching,—

> And if your minds are set upon me, and ye remember me as a father, permit no man to take my body and carry it into Egypt, lest, according to the custom which they have, they embalm me and lay me up in their houses, for it was [to avoid] this that I came into this desert. And ye know that I have continually made exhortation concerning this thing and begged that it should not be done, and ye well know how much I have blamed those who observed this custom. Dig a grave then, and bury me therein, and hide my body under the earth, and let these my words be observed carefully by you, and tell ye no man where ye lay me ; [and there I shall be] until the Resurrection of the dead, when I shall receive [again] this body without corruption.[2]

The corresponding passage in the Greek version is very similarly worded.[3]

Finally, Augustine in one of his sermons refers to Egyptian embalming in the following passage :—

---

[1] Budge : *The Paradise of the Fathers*, t. i, p. 382.
[2] Budge : *op. cit.*, t. i, p. 73.   [3] Migne, t. x, col. 2, p. 967.

HERODOTUS AND LATER AUTHORS

Now I beg of you not to bring against me the usual argument : " The bodies of those buried do not remain uncorrupted ; if they did, I could believe in their rising again." I suppose, then, that the only people who believe in the Resurrection are the Egyptians, who carefully preserve the bodies of their dead ! For they have a custom of drying them up, which makes them as durable as bronze. Are we to believe, then, according to those who know nothing of the hidden repositories in the universe, where all things are laid up for Him who placed them there, even when they have passed out of the ken of the mortal senses, that the Egyptians alone have true grounds for belief in the Resurrection of the Dead, and that the faith of all other Christians rests on a doubtful basis ? [1]

---

[1] Augustine : Sermo 361, *De Resurrectione Mortuorum* (= *De Diversis*, 120).

CHAPTER V

MUMMIFICATION IN THE OLD AND MIDDLE EMPIRES

WE are sadly hampered in our enquiries into the dawn of the art of mummifying through lack of material, but we may at once dispose of the notion that the predynastic Egyptians embalmed their dead. Many thousands of predynastic skeletons and naturally desiccated bodies have been examined from many sites in Egypt and Nubia by competent authorities. In none of these has the slightest trace of any preservative material whatever been found, nor has Dr. Schmidt, who has devoted the closest attention to the subject,[1] been able to detect any by means of chemical tests. The muscular tissues of these desiccated bodies often simulate resin, but the resemblance is utterly delusive. The skulls often contain particles which more than one writer has mistaken for resin or bitumen, but it has been proved that this material is really desiccated brain.[2] Nevertheless, there is the somewhat paradoxical fact that the body of an ancient Egyptian is hardly ever presented to us in a more excellent state of preservation than in some of the predynastic graves (such as those discovered by Dr. Reisner at Naga-ed-Dêr)—but preservation is the result, not of art, but of the operation of natural

---

[1] " Chemische und biologische Untersuchungen von ägyptischen Mumienmaterial," in the *Zeit. für allgemeine Physiologie*, Band VII, 1907, pp. 369–392.
[2] *Journ. Anatomy and Physiology*, vol 36, 1902, pp. 375–380.

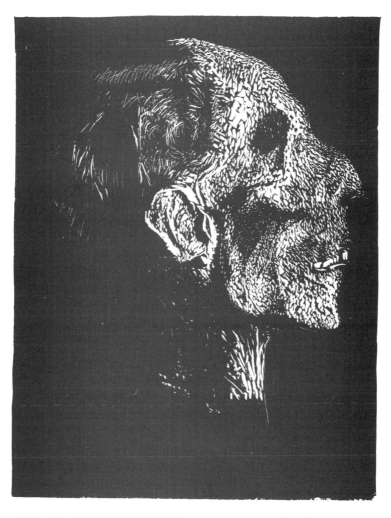

FIG. 22.—HEAD OF THE PHARAOH RAMESSES II   (XIXth DYNASTY)

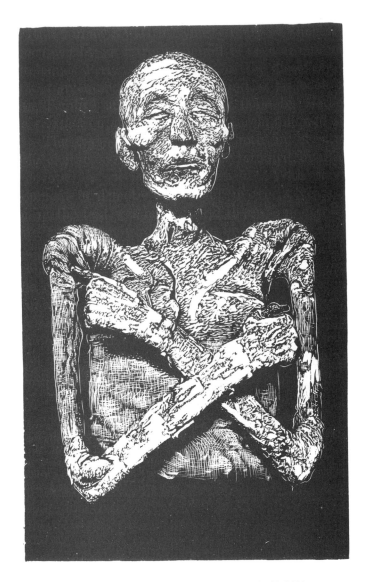

FIG: 23.—MUMMY OF THE PHARAOH MEÑEPTAH.
(XIXth DYNASTY)

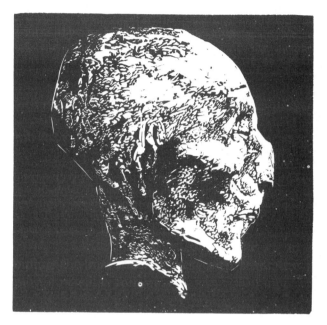

FIG. 24.—HEAD OF THE PHARAOH MENEPTAH (PROFILE)

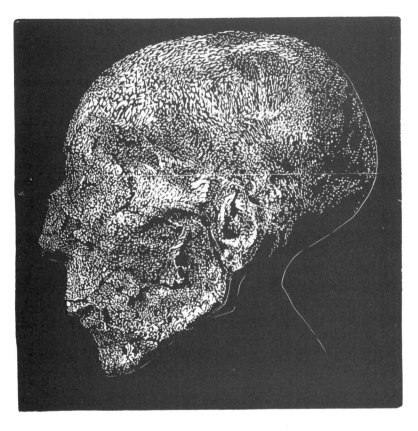

FIG. 25.—HEAD OF THE MUMMY OF SETY II ENCRUSTED WITH THE
RESINOUS PASTE USED BY THE EMBALMERS. (XIXth DYNASTY)

agencies. The corpses of these archaic people were placed directly in the dry sand and completely covered up, so as to shut out all access of air : as the result in many cases they became desiccated and perfectly preserved. Important as are the predynastic burials from the point of view of archæology and anthropology, they do not come within the scope of this book, as they are not true mummies, i.e. bodies embalmed and preserved by artificial means.[1]

The earliest embalmers had not acquired sufficient skill to render the bodies enduring, and as a result the mummies are so extremely fragile and perishable that none of such specimens is to be found in museums. As we have shown in Chapter I, there is strong presumptive evidence that mummification was attempted in the Ist Dynasty. The tombs of this age discovered at Nagada by De Morgan,[2] at Abydos by Petrie,[3] and at Naga-ed-Dêr by Reisner,[4] denote considerable elaboration of the funerary cult. The discovery in one of these tombs of the bones of a human arm, torn from a body, which was adorned with bracelets and wrapped in linen, has been claimed to support the view that mummification was attempted.[5] The predynastic custom of burying bodies in a flexed position persisted throughout the first three dynasties, the adoption of the extended position does not appear before the commencement of the Pyramid Age (IVth to VIth Dynasties).

During his excavations in the necropolis of Saqqara, in

---

[1] For large and valuable collections of material the reader is referred to the numerous publications which deal specially with predynastic burials, especially the works of Petrie, Reisner and the Reports of the Archæological Survey of Nubia.

[2] *Recherches sur les Origines de l'Egypte.*

[3] *Royal Tombs of the Earliest Dynasties* (2 vols., Eg. Expl. Fund).

[4] *Early Dynastic Cemeteries of Naga-ed-Dêr*, 2 vols., 1908–9.

[5] For this arm and its jewellery see Petrie : *Royal Tombs*, pt. ii, 1901, frontispiece.

a cemetery of the IInd Dynasty, Quibell discovered some human remains which seem to show that definite attempts at mummification had been made. One of these bodies, that of a woman of about thirty-five years of age (Fig. 1), was lying in a wooden coffin and was completely enwrapped in a complex series of bandages—more than sixteen layers still intact, and probably at least as many more destroyed : ten layers of fine bandage, then six layers of somewhat coarser cloth, and next to the body a series of much corroded, very irregularly woven cloth, much coarser than the outer layers. Each leg was wrapped separately. The body was flexed, as was usual at that period. In the wide interval between the bandages and the bones, there was a large mass of extremely corroded linen, whereas the intermediate and superficial layers were quite well preserved and free from corrosion, except along a line where the cloth was corroded to represent the *rima pudendi*—a fact of great interest when it is recalled that in the Vth, and probably IVth, Dynasties, it was the custom to fashion, in the case of male mummies, an artificial phallus. The corrosion is strong, presumptive evidence that some material (probably crude natron) was applied to the surface of the body in order to preserve it.[1]

Professor Garstang found similarly treated bodies, which he places between the IIIrd and IVth Dynasties, at Beni Hasan, but he did not recognise that any attempt at mummification had been attempted.[2]

Whilst excavating at Meidûm in 1891 Petrie discovered a very remarkable mummy, which he presented to the museum of the Royal College of Surgeons in London (Fig. 3), where we have recently re-examined it. The body is wrapped in large quantities of linen bandages of various textures.

[1] *Report*, British Association, Dundee 1912, p. 612.
[2] *Burial Customs of Ancient Egypt*, pp. 29–30 and fig. 18.

OLD AND MIDDLE EMPIRES

The outermost wrappings were saturated with resin, and the embalmers then moulded the mass carefully into shape, bestowing the minutest care to every detail of the form of the body. The details of the face, which is now somewhat distorted owing to the wrinkling of the linen and to the breakage of the nose in ancient times, are emphasised by paint, the eyes, eyebrows, and moustache being carefully traced. The resin-soaked linen set to form a carapace of stony hardness completely investing the whole head and body, and bulking it out to rather more than life-size. The generative organs are modelled with minute precision, and are so absolutely faithful to nature that it is hard to realise that they are merely represented by a linen and resin model. This mummy affords evidence that circumcision was practised. The body is lying in the fully extended position, which henceforth replaced the crouching attitude of earlier bodies, with the arms fully extended. The body-cavity is closely packed with resin-soaked linen.[1] The head (which has been broken from the trunk) rattles when shaken. Some free matter is therefore within the skull, but it is not possible to say whether this is desiccated brain or some artificial filling, though it is almost certainly the former.

The exact age of this mummy is uncertain. On archæological evidence it may be as early as the IIIrd Dynasty, but the extended position and the great advance in technique which it displays would seem to indicate a somewhat later date, probably Vth Dynasty. In any case it belongs to the Old Kingdom and is a wonderful testimony to the embalmers' skill in the Pyramid Age, and shows that they aimed at making a model or statue of the deceased out of, and whilst preserving, the actual tissues of his body.

---

[1] It is known that the viscera were removed at least as early as the IVth Dynasty, as canopic jars of that period are known.

EGYPTIAN MUMMIES

Professor Reisner's excavations in the Pyramid-field at Gizeh in 1913 brought to light a mummy of great interest. It was lying in a fully extended position in a rectangular, granite sarcophagus. Although plundered in ancient times, masses of linen bandaging remained. The embalming-incision is clearly visible in the customary position and was plugged with a large cake of resin, and the whole body, considering its great antiquity and the rough handling which it suffered at the hands of the plunderers, is in a wonderful state of preservation. Unfortunately no detailed description of this mummy has yet been published, but a photograph of it appeared in the excavators' report.[1] The whole treatment evidently resembles that of the Meidûm mummy.

In course of digging near the same site in the Old King-dom cemetery near the Great Pyramids, Professor Junker found a curious variation of the same method of procedure as that adopted in the Meidûm mummy, which he describes as follows : " In two graves we found the body covered with a layer of stucco-plaster, a method of treatment which is entirely peculiar. First of all the corpse was covered with a fine linen cloth, with the special purpose of preventing the mass of plaster from getting into the mouth, ears, nose, and so on. Then the plaster was put on and modelled according to the form of the body, the head being in one case so accurately followed that one can clearly see the fallen-in nose and twisted mouth. . . . In two further cases it was not the whole body that was covered with this layer of stucco, but only the head ; apparently because the head was regarded as the most important part, as the organs to taste, sight, smell and hearing were contained in it." [2]

---

[1] *Museum of Fine Arts Bulletin*, Boston, U.S.A., vol xi, No. 66, November 1913, p. 58.

[2] *Journal of Egyptian Archæology*, vol. i, p. 252.

Junker's interpretation takes no account of what was probably the strongest motive for this curious procedure, namely, the perpetuation of the dead man's identity by accurate preservation of his features. He connects the plastered masks with the "substitute heads" found in the tombs, to which we have already referred.

In the Cairo Museum is a mummy stated to be that of King Merenrē of the VIth Dynasty, found in his pyramid at Saqqara.[1] Although it was long ago shown that on the evidence of its technique the body cannot be older than the XVIIIth Dynasty,[2] the statement is still repeated.[3] This mummy is evidently an intrusive later burial. Exactly the same state of affairs is seen in the mummy, which is now in the British Museum, wrongly claimed to be that of Mykerinus of the IVth Dynasty, and found by Vyse in the third pyramid of Gizeh in 1837. The archæological evidence of the coffin and the technical evidence of the bones, again prove that we are dealing with a later intrusive burial. The Cairo Museum, however, contains a body which is certainly of the Vth Dynasty. It was discovered in the winter of 1897–8 by Petrie at Desasheh, and thus described by him in his report : [4] " Within lay the body on its back, head north, the head turned to the N.W. corner, and the feet far from the base. This seems as if the coffin had been lowered with the body in it, a tilt to one end having driven the body into that position. A stout, well-formed, but plainly made head-rest was set on end upon the breast. The sexual parts were modelled in cloth and placed in position. The whole body was fully wrapped up in linen, the skin and ligaments were firm and strong ; there was no sign of mummification in

---

[1] Maspero : *Guide du Visiteur*, ed. iv, 1915, p. 309.
[2] *Cairo Scientific Journal*, vol. ii, 1908, p. 205.
[3] Breasted : *History of Egypt*, 2nd ed., 1919, fig. 77.
[4] *Deshasheh*, p. 15.

this or other bodies in the cemetery, but only plain drying." The opinion that the body had been desiccated rather than embalmed is shared by Maspero,[1] but the treatment of the organs of reproduction and the preservation of the skin and ligaments would seem to indicate that the body had been prepared in the same way as (though less successfully than) the Meidûm and Gizeh mummies described above.

With the advent of the Middle Kingdom our material is somewhat more abundant. Many mummies of the XI–XIIIth Dynasties have been found from time to time, but with few exceptions they have either perished or been scattered to various museums in Europe and America without the publication of any adequate description.

Whilst excavating the XIth Dynasty temple at Deir-el-Bahari in the winter of 1906–7, Professor Naville discovered beneath the temple a series of tombs belonging to princesses of the period. Although they had all been plundered in antiquity, some interesting evidences of mummification were found. Unfortunately these have been distributed to several museums without any technical description of them having been published. One of them, which was broken to pieces, is now in the British Museum and is thus referred to in the report : [2] " The mummy, which was that of a woman, was in fragments. The skull (lower jaw missing), two feet and an arm, are now in the British Museum (Nos. 40924–7). The skull has pathological alterations ; a swelling of the bone on either side of the head, probably indicating a condition of inflammation before death. The feet and hands are very delicate, and the nails of the latter are carefully tinted

---

[1] *Guide du Visiteur*, ed. iv, 1915, p. 306, No. 3100.
[2] *The Eleventh Dynasty Temple of Deir-el-Bahari*, pt. i, p. 44. The arm and the feet are photographed on Pl. X of that work.

with henna." In another tomb, that of Princess Kemsit, a second mummy was found, "which had been stripped and roughly tied up again, was that of a woman and undoubtedly Kemsit herself. The head was twisted towards the left, as is usual in the XIth Dynasty . . . and, as we should expect from the paintings in the tomb, the skull is negroid in type." [1] Yet another of the princesses, Henhenit by name, was found in her tomb. " Her hands and feet are small and delicately formed, her hair short and straight. This is a very interesting mummy. It and the sarcophagus have been assigned to the Metropolitan Museum of New York." [2] A very small photograph of this mummy is given (in *op. cit.* Pl. X, Fig. 8), but unfortunately it shows the right side of the body, so that we are unable to say whether it had an embalming incision or not (Fig. 6). The body is fully extended with the hands on the thighs. The anterior abdominal wall is broken, the body-cavity being now apparently empty. The American expedition, working upon the same site about ten years later, discovered several other mummies of princesses of this period. This series of royal mummies of the XIth Dynasty from Deir-el-Bahari is of exceptional interest and importance to the student of the history of embalming. Unfortunately no exact data are yet available as to the technique adopted ; but we understand that, in some cases at least, no embalming-wound was found in either flank or in fact elsewhere. The preservation of the body seems to have been effected by a process mentioned by Herodotus. Resinous material was injected into the alimentary canal *per anum*. These mummies are interesting for another reason. Some of them are tattooed and represent not only the sole examples of tattooing yet

---

[1] *Op. cit.* pp. 49–50.
[2] These three brief reports are all we have by way of description.

EGYPTIAN MUMMIES

found in ancient Egyptian bodies,[1] but the earliest evidence of the practice anywhere.

Working near the Pyramids of Saqqara in the winter of 1906–7, Quibell discovered two interesting mummies of the early Middle Kingdom. Their fragile state made removal an impossibility, but opportunities were fortunately given for an examination, the report of which was published in the memoir recording the excavations.[2] The body (of Karenen) lay on its left side with its head to the north resting on a wooden pillow. Over the head was a cartonnage mask, with the wig painted green, the face yellow, and the moustache and beard green. The body was invested in great quantities of linen and an elaborate series of bandages. The arms, which were separately wrapped, were crossed on the breast, a posture which became customary in the late XVIIIth Dynasty, but is quite exceptional in early times. The hands were clenched. The whole body-cavity was filled with bundles of linen, on some of which incrustations of resin were clearly discernible. In the upper part of the thorax the remains of a viscus, probably the heart, were found. The embalming-wound was a fusiform gaping orifice in the usual position on the left flank. The penis was circumcised. Each leg was wrapped separately, the outermost wrappings being thickly encrusted with red resin. The inner wrappings, both on the limbs and body, were very much blackened and burnt, and were covered with salt crystals. The face was thickly smeared with resin, plugs of which were also placed in the nostrils. The eye-sockets were filled with plugs of linen, pushed in between the sunken eyes and the eyelids.

[1] A tattooed Nubian body of the same date has been recorded.
[2] Elliot-Smith *in* Quibell: *Excavations at Saqqara* 1906–7, Cairo 1908, pp. 13–14.

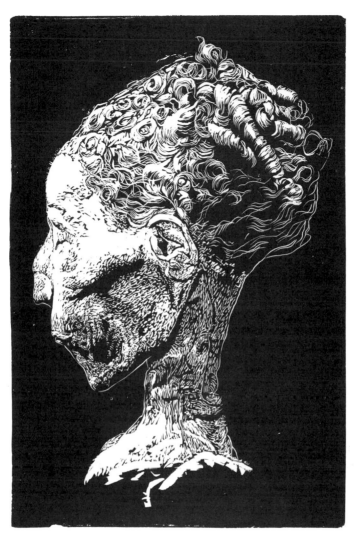

FIG. 26.—MUMMY OF AN UNKNOWN WOMAN (XIXth DYNASTY),
PROBABLY QUEEN TAUSRET

FIG. 27.—MUMMY OF THE PHARAOH RAMESSES III.
(XXth DYNASTY)

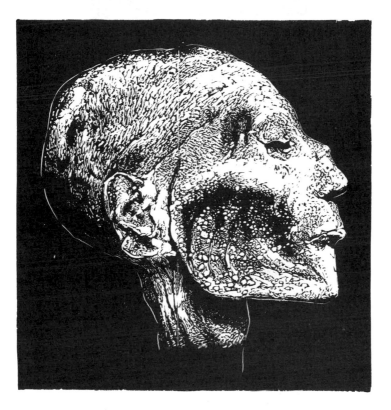

FIG. 28.—HEAD OF THE MUMMY OF RAMESSES V
Showing the eruption of the skin (probably small-pox)

FIG. 29.——HEAD OF THE MUMMY RAMESSES VI BROKEN TO
PIECES BY THE ANCIENT PLUNDERERS

The face bore a short, reddish moustache and beard of about two weeks' growth, and the short hair on the head was of the same colour. The other body, that of a woman, was not in such a good state of preservation. It apparently had been treated in the same way as the man's, but the fingers were extended and not clenched. It was possible to ascertain in both cases that the ethmoid bone was intact —another proof, if any were needed, that the custom of removing the brain through the nostrils is a product of a much later date.

An early XIIth Dynasty tomb discovered at Lisht by the American Expedition in the winter of 1906–7 contained a rich array of objects, amongst which were the much disintegrated remains of a mummy.[1] Enough remained, however, to show that the viscera had been removed through the usual embalming-wound, which was afterwards plugged with linen soaked in resin. The viscera were found in the four canopic jars. The body-cavity appears to have been packed with sawdust mixed with resin and with balls of linen, and the heart left *in situ* in the thorax. No attempt had been made to remove the brain or to pack the mouth or nose. A little resin was placed on the eyes, and the lids pulled down so as partly to conceal them. The viscera had been wrapped in linen parcels and embedded in some molten resinous matter poured into each of the canopic jars.

Amongst the smaller pit-tombs at Beni Hasan some very fruitful excavations were carried out by Professor Garstang in 1902–4, and a number of bodies was found. Curiously enough, Professor Garstang failed to recognise that mummi-

---

[1] The tomb and its contents are fully described in *The Tomb of Senebtisi* by Mace and Winlock, New York, 1916. The mummy is dealt with in the appendix by Elliot Smith.

fication had been practised—indeed he definitely states the contrary opinion.[1] He evidently looked for such evidence as we find in mummies of the New Kingdom and later, and does not allow for the fact that a very different technique was employed in the Middle Kingdom. The photograph of the head of Apa (*op. cit.* Fig. 177, p. 172) bears unmistakable evidence of artificial treatment. The photographs of the coffin and mummy of Userhēt show a method of burial exactly analogous to that of Senebtisi, and the inference is that the body was treated in the same manner.

The two mummies of the XIIth Dynasty discovered in a small tomb at Rifeh by Petrie, and now in the Manchester Museum, have been fully examined and described, and they afford valuable information as to the technical processes of mummification during the Middle Kingdom.[2] The use of the preserving-bath at this period is further demonstrated by the fact that the finger and toe-nails were tied on to the digits with thread to prevent them from coming away with the macerated epidermis during immersion. This procedure was followed throughout the New Kingdom (see p. 88). The bodies had been eviscerated, but owing to their fragile condition the body-wall had fallen in and no details of the embalming-incision could be observed, but the chest and abdomen had been packed with matting or coarse linen. The brain had not been extracted, and in one of the skulls a mass of desiccated brain was found. In the report on these two mummies a careful record of the bandaging is made and exhaustive anatomical and chemical reports are appended.

For the period intervening between the Middle and New

[1] *Burial Customs of Ancient Egypt*, p. 171.
[2] M. A. Murray and others : *The Tomb of Two Brothers*, Manchester 1910, pp. 31 ff.

OLD AND MIDDLE EMPIRES

Kingdoms, we have records of only two mummies.[1] This period, the length of which is so much in dispute between historians, corresponds to the time in which *rishi*-coffins (see below, p. 136) were in use. In the necropolis of Qurneh, near Thebes, Petrie found an undisturbed burial of this period, which he assigns to the XVIIth Dynasty, and of which he has given a full account.[2] The wrappings have been carefully recorded ; this is one of the few reliable accounts we have of the exact methods of swathing, which varied considerably from time to time. The body had almost entirely decayed, and very little could be learned from it. " Inside all [the bandages] the legs were wrapped separately, the arms, hands and fingers each wrapped separately diagonally. Pads of small cloths were used, but the whole was so much rotted by insects and decay, and loosened by the decay of all the flesh and shifting of bones, that the exact position could not be seen. Inside the stomach and pelvis was a thick mass of cloth squeezed in tightly, taking a mould of the whole hollow, 10 inches long, 7½ wide, 2½ thick. A large quantity of dark brown dust lay around the bones. The whole skeleton was perfectly preserved, the bones hard and greasy."[3]

The other mummy belonging to this period is that of Seknenrē, one of the last kings of the XVIIth Dynasty. This mummy is of very great interest, although it is not a normal one, for Seknenrē met his death either in battle or at the hands of assassins, the evidence for which we shall presently see from his skull. All that now remains of the king is a badly damaged, disarticulated skeleton, enclosed

---

[1] Three royal mummies of this period, those of two of the Antef Kings and of Queen Aahotpe, have been discovered in recent times (mid-nineteenth century) but all of them were destroyed.

[2] Petrie : *Qurneh*, pp. 6–10.   [3] *Op. cit.* p. 8.

in an imperfect sheet of soft, moist, flexible, dark-brown skin, which has a highly aromatic, spicy odour. The skin resembles that of mummies of the Coptic period after they have been exposed to the air and the preservative salts have deliquesced and softened the tissues. But by chemical tests Dr. W. A. Schmidt was unable to find in Seknenrē's skin any greater quantity of chloride of sodium than occurs in untreated human tissues. The spicy odour of the skin is due to the fact that it has been sprinkled with powdered aromatic wood or sawdust. No attempt was made to put the body into the customary mummy-position; the head had not been straightened on the trunk, the legs were not fully extended, and the arms and hands were left in the agonised attitudes into which they had been thrown in the death-spasms following the murderous attack, the evidence of which is so clearly impressed on the battered face and skull. Instead of being put into an attitude of repose, as was the usual custom in embalming, the face was left as it was found at the time of death, the lips widely retracted from the teeth, so that the mouth forms a distorted oval, the upper lip being pulled up towards the right, and the lower lip downward to the left. The whole attitude of the body is such as we might expect to find in the body of one who had suffered a violent death. Maspero reconstructed the death scene with great skill [1] and has also interpreted the state of the body, to which reference has just been made, as being clear evidence that it was hurriedly mummified, far away from the laboratories of the embalmers, probably on or near the field of battle. Dr. Fouquet [2] considered that the king had been killed on the field of battle, and that his mummy had been sent to Thebes for embalming,

---

[1] *Les Momies Royales*, p. 528.   [2] *Op. cit.* Appendix IV, p. 776.

and as the journey would have occupied some days, the body must have arrived in an advanced state of decomposition. The evidence is all against this view and favours Maspero's interpretation. The condition of the mummy is clearly not due to delay in being submitted to the embalmers, but to the manner of preserving the body—the method which remained in vogue in the XVIIIth Dynasty—and in this case it was performed in a rough and hasty manner. If the embalming had been done in a leisurely manner in Thebes, or in any other place where proper facilities existed, the mummy would certainly have received the usual careful preparation for wrapping, and the head and limbs would have been arranged in the customary way, and the face would have received its elaborate toilet after the manner of other mummies.

In the process of embalming a vertical incision was made in the left flank. This opening is now elliptical, and through it the greater part of the abdominal viscera had been removed. An opening large enough for the hand to pass through was likewise made in the diaphragm in order to remove the thoracic viscera. The abdomen, but not the thorax, was packed with linen, which had set into a solid mould with well-marked impressions of the embalming-wound and the hole in the diaphragm. Some portions of the viscera which had not been cleared out also adhered to this linen mass. No attempt had been made to remove the brain, nor were the extensive wounds in the skull used as a means of introducing any preservative or other matter into the cranium.

From an examination of the wounds on his skull, it is clear that Seknenrē met his death in an attack by at least two, and probably more, persons armed with weapons, one of which seems to have been an axe and the other a spear. The absence of any injuries to the arms or other parts of the body shows that no resistance could have been offered to the attack, and it is probable that the wounds were inflicted whilst Seknenrē was lying, perhaps asleep, on his right side. The anatomical details of the wounds and their positions and effects, by which the death-scene of this king can be fairly accurately reconstructed, have been worked out in detail elsewhere,[1] and it would be tedious to repeat them. This long-forgotten tragedy has left its mark for ever in a large gash in the frontal bone, in the hair matted with clotted blood, in another scalp wound which penetrated the frontal bone, in the broken bones of the nose, in the broken malar bone and orbit, in a spear-thrust immediately below the ear which smashed off the mastoid process, and was only prevented from doing further damage by the spear-point striking the atlas vertebra: in all these gruesome details, and in the expression of the face and the contortions of the body, is the vision of agony, which, once seen, is not easily forgotten.

[1] *The Royal Mummies*, pp. 4–6.

CHAPTER VI

MUMMIFICATION IN THE XVIIITH TO XXTH DYNASTIES

FROM the commencement of the XVIIIth Dynasty our material for the study of the technique of mummification becomes more abundant and chronologically continuous. The two great finds of royal mummies in 1881 and 1898 respectively have provided us with the bodies of most of the sovereigns of the New Empire, the most brilliant period in Egypt's eventful history. Wrecked and despoiled as they all are, we can nevertheless follow the embalmers' manipulations and study the progress of his craft, and by our observations on the technique of the mummies of the Pharaohs whose chronological position is known, we can date any other mummies which are anonymous or uninscribed and assign them to their proper places.

From the ill-preserved and fragile bodies of earlier periods which we considered in the previous chapter, we come to a series of mummies which show that the embalmers had devised a means of preserving their subjects in a fashion which was far more efficacious than that employed by their predecessors. From the time of Aahmosis I, the founder of the XVIIIth Dynasty, onwards, it became the invariable rule to remove the brain, a practice described by Herodotus, but of which there is no positive evidence prior to the XVIIIth Dynasty. Resinous paste was employed, which, on drying, imparted to the body a firmer consistency, rendering it much more enduring and preserving the integrity

87

of the skin. The saline bath was in use for immersion of
the body. In the steeping process the epidermis peeled off
and carried with it all the body-hair. The nails were
retained only because special precautions were taken to
prevent them from being dislodged. The head was apparently not immersed, for the epidermis and hair of the face
and scalp are usually intact. To prevent the loss of the nails,
the embalmers either tied them on to the fingers and toes,
or placed a metal thimble over the tip of the finger or toe
for the same purpose. Many of the mummies which have
been examined still have this thread, or well-marked impressions of it, and on some others thimbles have been
found. It may be mentioned that in widely-distant parts
of Africa embalmers paid particular attention to the
preservation of the nails.

The mummy of the Pharaoh Aahmosis I (Fig. 7) has a
hard carapace of resinous paste, the paste being smeared
so lavishly that the hair of the head is thickly matted, and
the embalming-wound in the left flank, through which the
viscera were removed, is not exposed for examination.
This mummy is of especial interest for the unusual manner
in which the brain was removed. Herodotus tells us that
the operation was performed through the nose with an iron
probe, and many mummies have been found in which this
method was evidently used. Greenhill, in his *History of
Embalming*, 1705, p. 249, speaks of such a method as a thing
" impracticable and amusing." Although tempted to agree
with Greenhill, Pettigrew [1] came to the conclusion after
examining a number of specimens, that such an operation
had been performed. A large series of mummies examined
in the Cairo School of Medicine in 1904 affords clear evidence

---

[1] *History of Egyptian Mummies*, 1834, pp. 44–6 and 53.

FIG. 30.—QUEEN NOZME. (XXIst DYNASTY)

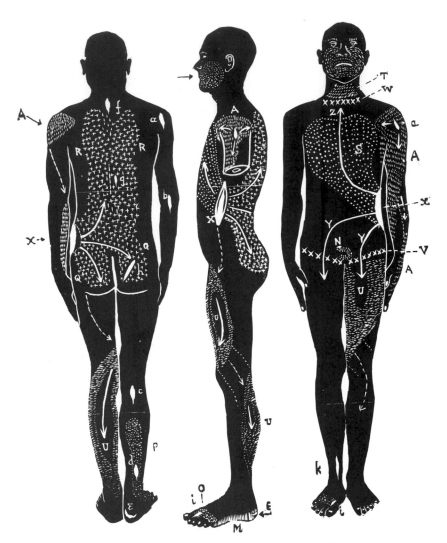

FIG. 31.—DIAGRAMS SHOWING THE PROCESS OF "PACKING" IN VOGUE IN THE
XXIst DYNASTY

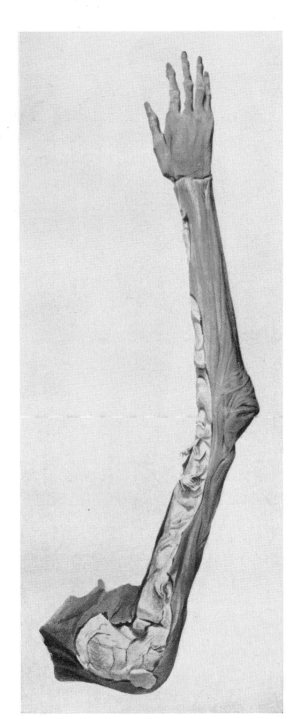

FIG. 32.—ARM OF A MUMMY OF THE XXIst DYNASTY, SHOWING THE PACKING MATERIAL. (THE OUTER SKIN HAS BEEN REMOVED)

FIG. 33.—HEAD OF THE MUMMY OF QUEEN HENTTAUI
(XXIst DYNASTY)

Showing the wig and artificial " packing " of the face

of the way in which the feat was performed.[1]   An instrument was forced up the nostril and driven right through the ethmoid bone.   Through this forced entrance into the cranial cavity the brain was removed piecemeal, probably by some small ladle-like instrument.   In most cases the whole of the brain was removed, but in some mummies fragments of the brain or its membranes remained in the skull.   The empty cavity was then packed with strips of linen soaked in resin.   Such was the usual method, but in the mummy of Aahmosis, a different procedure had been resorted to.   There is no distortion of the nose such as usually results from this operation, nor is the nasal septum damaged or in any way deflected.   As the cranial cavity was tightly packed with linen right down to the foramen magnum, it seems incredible that this could have been accomplished through the nasal fossæ without damage to the septum. Moreover, there is the curious and significant fact that the atlas vertebra is missing, and the upper surface of the axis and the neighbouring part of the occipital bone are thickly coated with resin, which must have been applied directly to the surface of the bones.   This raises the possibility that through an incision on the left side of the neck the atlas vertebra was excised and the brain extracted through the foramen magnum, the cavity being packed through the same opening with resin-smeared linen, which has in its passage coated the axis and occipital bone.   Such an operation would be one of great difficulty, and in spite of its apparent improbability, we are forced to accept it on the evidence adduced.   In no other known instance in Egypt has this method of procedure been followed, and it

---

[1] A technical description will be found in *Mém. Inst. Egyptien*, t. v, pp. 15 ff. (1906).   In the mummy of the boy found in the Tomb of Amenophis II (see below, p. 93) the perforation is made not in the ethmoid, but in the sphenoid bone.

would seem to indicate that it was an experimental beginning to what afterwards became general—the removal of the brain and the substitution of resinous material for it in the brain-case.

The arms are fully extended with the hands turned inwards at the sides of the thighs.

To about the same period belong several of the female mummies found at Deir-el-Bahari. The best preserved and most interesting is that of the lady Ray, who was nurse of Queen Nefretari, the consort of Aahmosis I. This mummy is one of the least unlovely of the series, and the lady in life must have been a graceful and delicate woman, with fine features and well-proportioned limbs. She still has abundant hair, arranged in small plaits, which are divided into two thick masses arranged on either side of the face, a form of hairdressing well known from the statues of the period (Figs. 8 and 9).

The whole body is sprinkled with a mixture of powdered resin and sand, and has the arms extended with the palms resting on the thighs. The hands are small and delicate and almost childlike in appearance. The embalming-wound is stuffed with a plug of linen and extends from the costal margin to the anterior superior spine of the ilium.

The mummy of Queen Nefretari shows that she was old at the time of her death, and her own very scanty locks are supplemented by twisting amongst them wisps of human hair in order to conceal a bald patch at the top of the head.

The mummy of Sitkamosis, daughter or sister of Aahmosis I, exhibits a more primitive form of treatment. One is therefore inclined to believe that she died some time before the king and was his elder sister and not his daughter. The brain has not been removed, but the position of the hands in front of the pubes was quite exceptional at the time of

Aahmosis, although it may have been customary before his mummy was prepared.

Amongst the mummies discovered at Deir-el-Bahari was one, which on account of its having been found in a coffin bearing the name of Pinozem I of the XXIst Dynasty, was formerly supposed to be the mummy of that king. Maspero, however, formed the opinion that it was the mummy of Tuthmosis I on account of the facial resemblance which it bore to the Pharaohs Tuthmosis II and III.[1] The technique of mummification displayed in this specimen, as well as the position in which the arms are placed, indicates that the body was embalmed at a period earlier than that of Tuthmosis II, and later than that of Aahmosis I. The mummy of Amenophis I is in the Cairo Museum, and has not been unrolled (see Fig. 45), so that the only vacant place amongst the kings to be filled is that of Tuthmosis I. The body is well preserved, although the thick plastering of resinous paste which was used at the beginning of the dynasty is not employed and the hands are placed in front of the pubes, both of which are signs of later rather than earlier date.[2]

With the mummy of Tuthmosis II some new features of treatment are revealed. The arms are crossed upon the breast, a custom which remained in vogue until the extended attitude was revived in the XXIst Dynasty. The orifices of the ears are plugged with round balls of resin, which are *in situ*. Although missing from the mummy of Tuthmosis I, there is evidence that these plugs had been employed in the case of his mummy also.

Between this mummy and that of Tuthmosis III must

---

[1] *Struggle of the Nations*, p. 242. *Les Momies Royales*, pp. 545, 581, 582.
[2] The chronological position of this mummy in the series is fully discussed, and a considerable amount of detail considered, in *The Royal Mummies*, pp. 25–27.

be placed the well-preserved body of an unknown man (Fig. 11). The body was formerly supposed to be that of the scribe Nebseni, because it was found in a coffin bearing that name. As the coffin is of XXth Dynasty date, and the mummy is unquestionably of early XVIIIth Dynasty date, the identity cannot be maintained.

The mummy of the Pharaoh Tuthmosis III had been greatly maltreated by the robbers, and in restoring it the priests of the XXIst Dynasty had strengthened the body by four large splints, which were wooden oars belonging to the burial equipment. The treatment of the mummy is consistent with the period, but the hands, which were crossed on the breast, were clenched in the attitude of grasping some object, doubtless a ceremonial whip and a sceptre which the robbers had stolen. In this mummy a difference in the site of the embalming-wound is revealed, and the new fashion remained in vogue until the end of the XXth Dynasty. Instead of the vertical incision from the lower margin of the ribs to the anterior spine of the hip-bone, an oblique cut was made from near the latter point towards the pubes.

The skull of this Pharaoh is very remarkable for its large capacity, and it is of pentagonoid form. The face is small, narrow and elliptical. If one restores the facial features of this damaged mummy, a contour strikingly like the Deir-el-Bahari portrait and the beautiful statue in the Cairo Museum [1] will be obtained.[2]

The mummy of Amenophis II lies in his own tomb in the Valley of the Kings.[3] The arms were crossed upon the

---

[1] Legrain : *Statues et Statuettes* (Cairo Mus. Catalogue), Pl. XXX, No. 42053, Cairo 1906.

[2] See the diagram in *The Royal Mummies*, p. 35.

[3] A photograph of the mummy lying in its sarcophagus will be found in *Wonders of the Past*, vol. i, p. 394.

breast, but the forearms are nearly parallel and placed lower down than was usual, and the fingers were not tightly clenched.   When this king was found in his tomb in 1898, he was accompanied by a number of other royal mummies which had been deposited in his tomb in ancient times for safety.   All had been maltreated by the robbers, and some of them belong to a considerably later period.   The mummies of two women and a boy, however, are probably contemporary. The elder woman (Figs. 12 and 13) is middle-aged, but with long, brown, wavy, lustrous hair parted in the centre and falling down on both sides of the head on to the shoulders. The right arm is extended with the hand resting on the thigh, but the left hand is tightly clenched, the forearm being bent at the elbow so that the hand is placed just over the top of the breast-bone.   As was customary in mummies of this period of both sexes, the perineum is covered with a thick cake of resinous paste.   The mummy of the boy is of great interest.   The hair has been shaved from the greater part of the scalp, but on the right side of the head it is left uncut, and forms a long, wavy, lustrous tress, and from its waviness we may infer that it was originally plaited (Fig. 16).   This is the well-known " Horus-lock," worn by young princes in honour of the god, and which is often represented in statues and bas-reliefs.   It may also be noted that this boy, who is about eleven years of age, is not circumcised, although circumcision was regularly practised in Egypt [1] and all the male mummies from the earliest times afford evidence of the custom.   The hands are placed in front of the pubes, the right hand with extended fingers, the left hand being clenched.   This position of the arms, like that of the next mummy to be mentioned, is a reversion

---

[1] See Capart : *Une Rue de Tombeaux*, Pl. LXVI, where the ceremony is being performed.

EGYPTIAN MUMMIES

to the custom which prevailed before the time of Tuthmosis II. The large aperture in the chest is the work of the tomb-robbers.

The younger woman from the same tomb (Figs. 14 and 15) was formerly believed to be that of a man, because the head was closely shaven, but the anatomical evidence of sex is quite certain. It was possible to ascertain from this mummy that the diaphragm had not been removed, but had been perforated to allow the lungs to be extracted, the heart being left intact.[1]

The mummy of Tuthmosis IV is that of a young, extremely emaciated man, with a long, oval, effeminate face (Fig. 17). The body is well preserved and has the arms crossed on the breast. The condition of the mummy raises many interesting anatomical problems bearing on the evidence of ossification in the determination of age.[2]

The mummy of Amenophis III was smashed to pieces by the plunderers, a fact which is particularly regrettable because there are evidences of quite a special procedure in embalming. In spite of its shattered condition, it is still possible to observe that the embalmers had taken great pains to restore to the shrunken body something of the form and plumpness it possessed during life. This was accomplished by stuffing under the skin of the legs, arms and neck a mass of resinous material, which was moulded into form, so that, when dry, the skin set firmly upon a stony-hard mould. This procedure foreshadows a method which became customary and developed as a fine art in the XXIst Dynasty (see Chapter VII), but is the only known instance of it before that time. It may be noted that, from

[1] The significance of the heart will be referred to later. (See pp. 145.)
[2] Fully dealt with in *The Royal Mummies*, pp. 44–45. This mummy is the only one so far that has been examined with X-rays.

the condition of the teeth, it is evident that the king must have suffered acutely from toothache, as there were extensive alveolar abscesses.

Amenophis IV, afterwards called Akhenaten, the great religious reformer, and the founder of the City of Akhetaten (the modern Tell-el-Amarna), was the most interesting king that ever occupied the throne of Egypt. The peculiar shape of his head and body as represented by contemporary artists would have made his mummy one of particular interest and importance for examination. The irony of events has denied us the possibility of making such an examination, for after his death at his new city of Akhetaten, his body was moved to Thebes and placed in a tomb which was thought to be that of his mother, Queen Tiyi.[1] Owing to a defect of the rock in which the tomb had been hewn, water had penetrated, and caused the coffin to rot and collapse upon the body within it, doing irreparable damage. It may be mentioned in passing that this coffin, when complete, must have been one of the finest ever made in Egypt ; it is incrusted with enamel and coloured stones, and was a work of rare beauty. Its shattered fragments have been removed to the Cairo Museum and an attempt has been made to restore it. The mummy had not been plundered, but was found in its original wrappings, encircled by bands of gold.[2] As in the case of the mummy of Tuthmosis IV, the anatomical evidence of age is of the greatest importance, and the technical evidence on this point has been fully dealt with elsewhere.[3]

If Akhenaten had been a normal individual the condition

---

[1] An account of the discovery and of the objects found in the tomb will be found in *The Tomb of Queen Tiyi* (Theodore M. Davis' excavations, London 1910).

[2] See *Journal of Eg. Arch.*, vol. 8, pp. 193 ff.

[3] *The Royal Mummies*, pp. 52–3.

of his skeleton would have forced us to the conclusion that his age at the time of death was probably about twenty-five or twenty-six years, with just a possibility that he might have been as old as thirty years. It is difficult to bring such an estimate into strict conformity with the known historical facts,[1] although perhaps not altogether impossible. The peculiar configuration of Akhenaten's body, as depicted in his statues and bas-reliefs, suggests the possibility that he may have suffered from a rare affection, one of the effects of which is to delay the consolidation of the bones ; so that the condition of the skeleton found in the normal individual at twenty-five years might be retained as much as ten years longer.[2] The slight degree of hydrocephalus revealed in the actual skull lends some support to this suggestion. In addition it helps to explain the peculiar traits of face and head in the contemporary portraits of Akhenaten.

The true solution of the problem, however, is fraught with difficulties, some of which could be eliminated by a thorough examination of his bones, which circumstances made it impossible to carry out when one of us was preparing his report upon them in 1907. While there is no doubt that the peculiar form of Akhenaten's skull was due in the main to pathological causes, the configuration of the heads of his daughters (as revealed in their portrait statues) is susceptible of another explanation.[3] Either they were not true to nature (in which case they may have been grossly exaggerated expressions of the form in which Akhenaten's infirmities were conventionally portrayed), or the children's heads had been subjected during their infancy to the kind

---

[1] Kurt Sethe : *Beiträge zur Geschichte Amenophis IV, Nachrichten d. K. Gesellsch d. Wissensch zu Göttingen*, Phil. Hist. Kl., 1921.

[2] G. Elliot Smith : *Tutankhamen*, 1923, p. 83.

[3] See especially the fine coloured drawing of these princesses in the *Journal of Egyptian Archæology*, vol. vii, Pl. I.

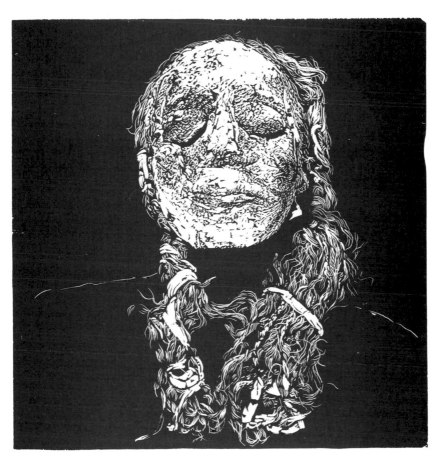

FIG. 34.—MUMMY OF PRINCESS NESIKHONS. (XXISt DYNASTY)

Showing the protective disks over the eyes

FIG. 35.—MUMMY OF PRINCESS NESITANEBASHER. (XXISt DYNASTY)
Showing the artificial eyes and " packing " of the face and neck

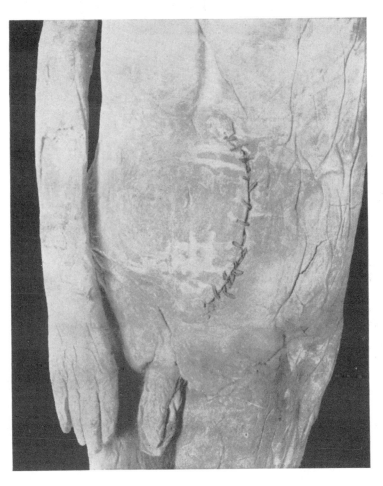

FIG. 36.—EMBALMING-WOUND OF A XXISt DYNASTY MUMMY SEWN
UP WITH STRING

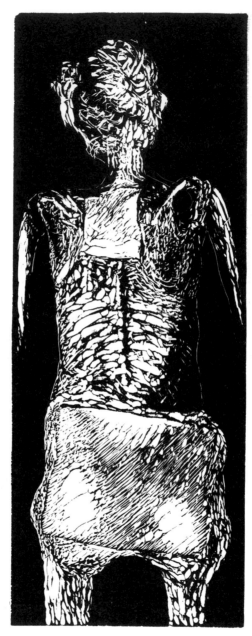

FIG. 37.——MUMMY OF AN OLD WOMAN OF THE
XXIst DYNASTY

Showing the patches of gazelle-skin fixed by
the embalmers to cover bed-sores

of artificial deformation that is said to have been practised in Asia Minor even in times as early as Akhenaten's reign.

This question cannot be decided until we recover the mummy of Tutankhamen's queen, or of one of her sisters.

A remarkable discovery made in the Valley of the Kings in 1905 has provided us with the mummies of Yuaa and Thuiu, the parents of Queen Tiyi, Akhenaten's wife.[1] (See Figs. 18–20.)

The mummy of Yuaa is that of a white-haired old man, with thick wavy hair, now stained yellow by the embalming materials (Fig. 18). The body was embalmed in the usual manner of the period, and no attempt was made to pack it as in the case of Amenophis III. The body-cavity was filled with balls of coarse linen soaked in resin, which is now a hard solidified mass. The perineum is coated with resin so thickly as to conceal the genital organs ; this method was employed in the mummies of Amenophis II and of three other contemporary mummies found in his tomb.[2] The arms are crossed high on the chest, and the extended fingers reach nearly to the chin. As was usual in the XVIIIth Dynasty, the eye-sockets were packed with linen over the shrunken orbits, and the eye-lids pulled down over this packing material. The whole aspect of the face is one of great dignity and repose, and the mummy is the finest specimen we possess of the XVIIIth Dynasty— unless the mummy of Tutankhamen proves to excel it.

Yuaa's wife Thuiu was found in her husband's tomb, and is another excellent example of the perfection to which the embalmer's art had been brought at the end of the

---

[1] For an account of the discovery and of the remarkable array of objects found in the tomb, see Quibell, *The Tomb of Yuaa and Thuiu* (Cairo 1908), in which one of us has described the mummies.

[2] *Bulletin de l'Inst. Eg.*, 5th series, t. i, p. 224.

XVIIIth Dynasty (Figs. 19, 20). The mummy presented some unusual features for its period. The embalming-wound is almost vertical and was sewn up with string, a quite exceptional feature at this time,[1] and the arms are fully extended with the palms on the thighs—both these details being a reversion to the customs of the earlier part of the dynasty. Some attempt seems to have been made to represent artificial eyes by painting the packing material under the eyelids. Another peculiar feature of this mummy is the fact that upon the feet sandals (made of mud) were placed. The soles are of metal, and the straps had apparently been gilded. Thuiu was a little old woman, very bald on the crown of the head, her scanty locks being wound about the temples. The breasts were shrunken and characteristically senile.

Of the kings of the XIXth Dynasty the mummies of many have survived. The first king of the dynasty was Haremhab, and his tomb was discovered by Theodore Davis in 1908. In the sarcophagus were the remains of a mummy, but what became of it is unknown. In spite of what Mr. Davis has written in the volume dealing with this tomb, the bones were not submitted to any examination at the time of their discovery. The next king, Ramesses I, has likewise escaped us, but his son, Sety I, lies in the Cairo Museum. There is nothing in the mode of treatment of this mummy to distinguish it from that in vogue at the latter part of the XVIIIth Dynasty. The head is in a fine state of preservation (Fig. 21), and reveals to us one of the most perfect examples of manly dignity displayed in a mummy that has come down to us from ancient Egypt, but the body has suffered considerably at the hands of the

---

[1] Sewing was practised in the XXth and XXIst Dynasties (see pp. 100 and 119).

plunderers. The body-cavity and chest were packed with resin-soaked linen, and there is evidence that the heart, as was customary, was left *in situ*.

Ramesses II, until Tutankhamen displaced him, was the best-known and most famous of all the Pharaohs. He had a long reign (over sixty years), and was a very old man, perhaps a centenarian, at the time of his death. The temples and the back of the head are covered with fine, silky hair, which originally must have been quite white but is now yellow. The upper part of the scalp was quite bald, although there are still scanty hairs on the frontal region (Fig. 22). Amongst them are some " blackheads," due to the plugging of the orifices of the sluggish sebaceous glands, a condition frequent in old men. The superficial temporal arteries are very prominent and tortuous, and their walls are calcareous. On the vertex, near the extremity of the greatly enlarged anterior branch of the right superficial temporal artery, there are curious markings upon the bald scalp. There is a well-marked white line, running in the mesial sagittal plane, and a fainter transverse mark, forming a cross-like pattern.

Ramesses II had a low, sloping forehead and a prominent nose. His mummy reveals a distinct advance in the technique of embalming ; for the first time it became possible to preserve the skin without the dark brown or black discoloration that occurred invariably in earlier attempts at mummification. It is very remarkable that the teeth are all healthy and only slightly worn, in spite of the Pharaoh's extreme old age. Nearly all the royal mummies, even those of young men, have well-worn teeth, and in many cases they suffered from severe dental caries and from alveolar abscesses.

His son and successor, Meneptah, the reputed Pharaoh of the Exodus, is likewise an old man. The physical characters bear close affinity with those of Sety I and Ramesses II. The mummy is well preserved and is similar in technique to that of Ramesses II in that the general darkening of the skin has been avoided (Figs. 23 and 24). A curious feature of this mummy is the entire absence of the scrotum, but it is not possible to say definitely whether the castration occurred before or after death. It was certainly done before the process of embalming was completed, as the wound is smeared with balsam ; but if the injury was inflicted before death, the existence of the open wound shows that it was recent. The hands were placed in the position of grasping sceptres, and the skin of the body is thickly encrusted with salt. It is curious that there is a hole in the back of the skull, a feature also seen in the mummies of Sety II, Ramesses IV, V and VI. Maspero considered this to have been done by the embalmers in order to allow evil spirits a free exit from the head. It may have been done for this reason, but it may be the work of ancient plunderers who inflicted severe damage on all these mummies when, with an axe, the wrappings of the head were hastily chopped away.

The mummy of Siptah had been badly damaged and the priests who restored it refixed the broken forearm in a splint. Siptah had " club-foot," a point which will be referred to again. (See p. 157 and Fig. 65.) The body-cavity was stuffed with lichen instead of the usual linen filling, and the embalming-wound was sewn up with a strip of linen, a custom which was maintained until the time of Ramesses IV, when it was generally abandoned, but occasionally revived in the XXIst Dynasty.

Siptah's successor, Sety II, had been successfully mummified and wrapped in great quantities of exceptionally fine linen of gauzy texture. The body, like most of the others, had been very badly treated by the ancient robbers, who had smashed off the arms, damaged the trunk and severed the head, and, when found, the right hand and forearm were missing. This mummy was clothed in two remarkable shirts, which are referred to again below, p. 142. Siptah was the last king of the XIXth Dynasty, and his successor, Setnakht, inaugurates the XXth Dynasty and was succeeded by nine Pharaohs, all bearing the great name of Ramesses.

Setnakht's mummy has not been found, but the lid of his coffin, turned face-downwards, was used as an improvised shell for the accommodation of the mummy of an unknown woman, who was found with the batch of royal mummies in the Tomb of Amenophis II in 1898 (Fig. 26).

On the sole of each foot there was a large mass, wrapped in coarse cloth, and fixed in position by bandages of the leg which passed around it. The parcel on the right foot contained a mass of epidermis mixed with large quantities of natron ; that on the left portions of viscera with similar preservative material. The epidermis had been removed from the soles of the feet for the most part and the small remaining fragment had a clean-cut edge. After removing a series of bandages from the head, some of which had been wound in a circular manner and others forming a figure-of-eight around the head and neck, the hair was found to be enclosed in cloths tied like those of modern Egyptian girls. A piece of linen about the size of an ordinary handkerchief was placed upon the head and its lateral corners brought round to the forehead and tied in a knot. Neither the fingers nor the toes were wrapped separately. The arms were placed vertically at the sides, the hands being upon the lateral surfaces of the thighs. The mummy had escaped all damage at the hands of tomb-robbers, excepting that a large rounded hole had been made through the brittle anterior abdominal wall in the epigastrium. The second and third toes of the left foot were bent sharply upward ; but this had been done when the body was still plastic.

The body is that of an extremely emaciated woman with atrophied breasts. Her hair is well preserved and has been made into a series of sharply rolled curls, of the variety distinguished by modern ladies by the name " Empire " (Fig. 26). She had a prominent, narrow, high-bridged, " Ramesside " nose ; but the pressure of the bandages has distorted the cartilaginous part and marred its beauty. She had a straight line of brow, and a long hanging jaw. The packing of the mouth has given the lips a pouting expression and further disturbed the natural profile of the face. There is a large widely gaping elliptical embalming-wound placed obliquely, with its long axis parallel to Poupart's ligament. It extends as far as the symphysis pubis below to beyond the anterior superior spine of the hip-bone above. A large pad of linen had been pushed against the perineal region—not the perineum proper, so much as the neighbourhood of the obturator foramina—producing large depressions at the inner side of each femoral neck. There was no sign of any writing or any inscription that might indicate the identity of this woman.

The complete absence of any attempt at packing the limbs or trunk, and the situation of the embalming-wound, demonstrate that the body was mummified before the beginning of the XXIst Dynasty. The texture of the tissues, the light colour of the skin, and the absence of any of the discoloration that was the rule up till the time of Sety I, and other details of the embalmer's technique indicate that this body was not mummified before the latter part of the XIXth Dynasty.

The position of the arms gives us no information, for the conventions adopted in the case of men did not apply to women. At all periods the mummies of women had their hands alongside the thighs, although there were occasional exceptions to this rule (as for example the elder woman in Amenophis II's tomb). The nature and situation of the embalming-wound varies a good deal from reign to reign. In this mummy it is placed alongside Poupart's ligament, as was customary in the latter part of the XVIIIth Dynasty. But the state of preservation of the mummy puts this period out of the question. In the early part of the XIXth Dynasty it was the rule to extend the embalming-wound upwards into the iliac region ; but at the close of that Dynasty (in the mummies of Siptah and Sety II) the embalmers returned to the late XVIIIth Dynasty convention, as in this mummy ; and in the XXth Dynasty (Ramesses IV and V) the early XIXth Dynasty (Ramesses II and Menephtah) site once more becomes the fashionable one. In the XXIst and XXIInd Dynasty the early XVIIIth Dynasty site (high or suprailiac incision) comes into vogue. Thus on the evidence of the site of the embalming-incision one might be inclined to put this mummy into the same group as Siptah's and Sety II's. But in the case of both of these mummies, as well as in that of Ramesses IV (it is not known how the wound was treated in Ramesses III), the incision was stitched up, whereas it is gaping in this woman's mummy. However, two mummies of the same date (for instance, Yuaa's and Thuiu's) may be treated in different ways. Then again, there is the nature of stuffing material in the body-cavity— the use of strips of linen. Sety II had hard resin-impregnated linen, like the XVIIIth Dynasty mummies, whereas Siptah and Ramesses IV had dried lichen. From this it seems that the end of the XIXth and the commencement of the XXth Dynasties represent a transition period when experiments were being made in new forms of packing material. In the mummy under consideration ordinary linen bandages, not treated with resin, were employed. The fact that no attempt was made to make artificial eyes favours the view that the mummy was earlier than Ramesses IV, although this kind of evidence is not altogether conclusive, as the mummy of Ramesses V shows. On the other hand, the practice of stuffing the cheeks does not begin until the time of Siptah, so far as we are aware.

The evidence is quite conclusive that this mummy belongs to the XIXth–XXth epoch, and there is a good deal to suggest that it was either very late XIXth or very early XXth. The fact that it was associated with a group of mummies of kings suggests that this lady was also a member of the royal family. It is a very suggestive fact that the only woman's tomb of the XIXth–XXth date that is known in the Bibân-el-Molûk was made for Tausret, the consort in succession of Siptah and Sety II, to whose times the technique of the mummification has led us to assign this body.

This mummy has been described at considerable length in order to illustrate the indications which we must look for in order to date a mummy from technical evidence alone, when there is no inscription or other archæological clue to guide us. In the case of the next one, however, that of Ramesses III, we are on sure ground again (Fig. 27).

As the resin-impregnated linen carapace investing this mummy is quite complete excepting the head portion, which was removed in 1886, it was deemed undesirable to interfere with it. Hence we have no direct information concerning the treatment of the body of Ramesses III ; but the details of the embalmer's technique were so similar in the late XIXth (as revealed in the mummies of Siptah and of Sety II) and the XXth Dynasty (as seen in Ramesses IV and his successors), that it is unlikely that this mummy would have thrown any new light upon the methods of mummification. It would have been of interest to learn whether any protecting plate was placed over the embalming-

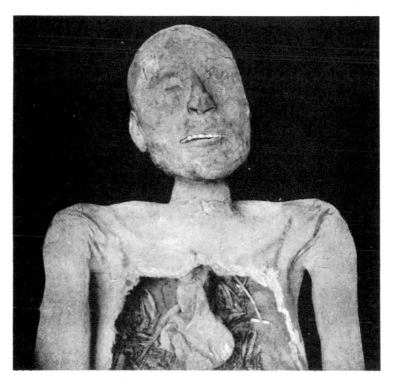

FIG. 38.—MUMMY OF A PRIEST OF AMEN (XXIst DYNASTY) WITH THE
CHEST WALL REMOVED TO SHOW THE HEART AND AORTA LEFT
IN SITU

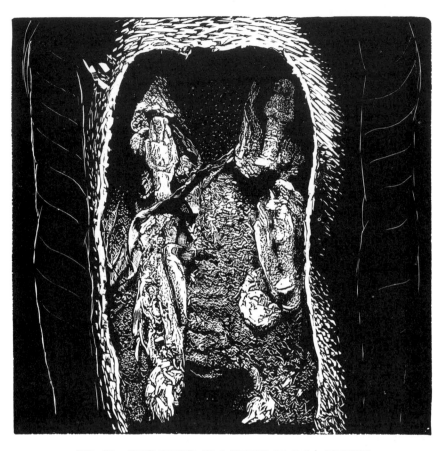

FIG. 39.—BODY-CAVITY OF A MUMMY OF XXIst DYNASTY

Showing the four parcels of viscera with wax figures of their protective genii

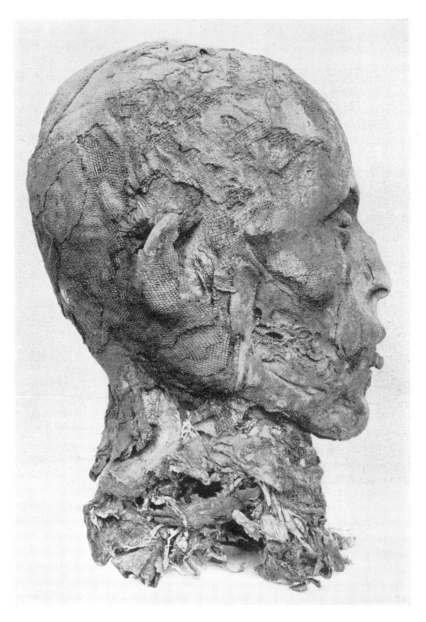

FIG. 40.—HEAD OF A PTOLEMAIC MUMMY FROM NUBIA

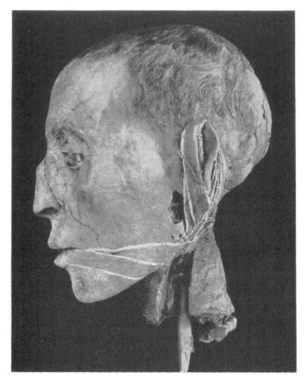

FIG. 41.—HEAD OF A PTOLEMAIC MUMMY ACCIDENTALLY SEVERED FROM THE BODY AND REFIXED ON A STICK AND TIED WITH BANDAGES.

FIG. 42.—MASS OF RESIN FROM THE THORAX OF THE MUMMY OF A YOUNG WOMAN WITH INSECTS EMBEDDED IN IT. (PTOLEMAIC PERIOD)

wound ; and if so, whether it was of the oblong form (with the symbolic eye engraved upon it) as in the XXIst Dynasty, or the plain leaf-like form used in the XVIIIth Dynasty. The use of X-rays would settle matters for this as for many other mummies. There are, however, several features that may be regarded as innovations. The hands, for instance, are not flexed as in the mummies of the late XVIIIth and XIXth Dynasties, but are fully extended with the palms resting upon the shoulders. As the full extension of both hands, in association with flexed elbows, occurs also in the mummies of Ramesses IVth Vth and (probably) VIth, but in no other mummies, it can be regarded as a distinctive feature of XXth Dynasty mummification, which passed out of use before the commencement of the XXIst Dynasty, for the " Leeds Mummy," which was embalmed in the reign of Ramesses XI, has the arms extended with the hands over the pubic region.[1] Again, in this mummy, artificial eyes are employed for the first time.

The mummy of Ramesses IV is that of an elderly man, probably about fifty years of age. It is well preserved and covered (except for the head) in a thick layer of resinous paste. For artificial eyes small onions were used, and they give a surprisingly realistic effect. This mummy, like those of Meneptah, Sety II, Ramesses V and Ramesses VI, has an irregular hole in the top of the skull, a point to which we have already referred. This mummy, so far as the positions of the embalming-wound and arms are concerned, conforms to the custom of the times. It presents one new feature, namely the plugging of the anus with a ball of resin.

Ramesses V was a thin, emaciated man and probably a physical weakling. The face and the pubic region are

---

[1] *Account of an Egyptian Mummy presented to .   the Leeds Philosophical and Literary Society*, by W. Osburn.   Leeds, 1828.

thickly studded with papular eruptions, probably small-pox (Fig. 28), and there is evidence that he suffered from inguinal hernia. He also had a large ulcer in the right groin.

The most tragic instance of mutilation by tomb-robbers is seen in the mummy of Ramesses VI. All the royal mummies had been badly damaged by plunderers, but this one was literally hacked to pieces. The priests who in ancient times visited his plundered tomb, must have found the mummy scattered in fragments on the floor. They made up a bundle, exteriorly quite a presentable mummy, of the pieces and placed them in a coffin. As an instance of how such material has to be dealt with, we will describe it in detail.

The shroud of fine linen, which had enveloped the whole body, was already pulled aside from the upper part of the mummy, where the underlying wrappings were in a state of great disorder.

Amongst the mass of rags the broken pieces of the head and a woman's right hand came to light. In removing the loose bundle of torn pieces of linen that were thrown around the chest, a distorted and mutilated right hand and forearm of a man were found, but they did not belong to this mummy. In the place where the neck of the mummy should have been was the separate left hip-bone (os innominatum) and the rest of the pelvis. The right elbow and the lower half of the humerus were found lying on the right thigh and the head of the left femur was alongside the upper end of this fragment in front of the abdomen.

When the bandages investing the right thigh were removed the right forearm (hacked off at the elbow and wrist with axe-cuts) was found—still wrapped in its original bandages. Although an attempt had thus been made to put the arm into the position in which it was customary to place it at the time the rewrapping was done (i.e. vertically

106

at the sides—the XXIst Dynasty custom), it is interesting to note that the folds of skin around the elbow make it clear that the arms were originally folded over the chest, as the practice was in the XXth Dynasty. The left upper arm was torn off at the shoulder and put in its proper place. The rest of the arm had been chopped off at the elbow. On removing the first bandage, which passed spirally around the lower parts of the legs, a broken piece of rib was found lying in front of the ankles. This bandage was a tattered strip of fine linen 3 m. 005 mill. by 0 m. 19 cent. A second similar bandage passed spirally around the legs upward beyond the knees and a third continued the process upward to the hips.

A mass of loose rags was then removed from the front of the knees. Then was exposed a longitudinal sheet of very coarse matting tied in front of the legs by irregular scraps of fine linen in the form of circular ligatures. When this was removed a series of short bandages of varied materials and sizes was found—but all of them old tattered scraps— wound spirally around the legs. Then a mass of loose rags was found packed around the left hand and forearm. There was then exposed a complicated bandage intended to fix the head and the other loose fragments to the legs—the only coherent parts of the body. A yellowish shawl was slung round the thighs fixing the left forearm ; it was looped in front and then passed obliquely downward, then under the feet and up as far as the right knee, where it was tied to a reddish-brown scarf, which passed right up around the fragments of the head, down the left side of the body and under the feet, reaching almost as far as the above-mentioned knot.

When this was removed three bandages were found fixing the legs to the board on which the mummy was placed : a figure-of-eight around the ankles and feet, a circular bandage below the knees and another around the thighs. Then a peculiar sheet of linen—apparently the remains of a dress, with two armholes—was wrapped around the mummy. The ends of the sheet (for one third of the distance at each end) were torn into four strips of equal breadth : at the head-end the outer pair of tails were torn off and the remaining two were tied around the head. The tails at the other end were wrapped in figures-of-eight around the legs. Under these, two bandages were found—one passing in a circular manner around the hips and the other around the ankles. After removing a few loose rags the remains of the body were exposed. The separated anterior abdominal wall was turned inside out. The neck was severed from the body at the sixth cervical vertebra. The lower jaw and the skin covering it were detached from the head. The whole facial skeleton was broken off and lost, only the skin of the face remaining. There is a large gash caused by two axe-cuts just above the left ear and temporo-maxillary joint, and a second vertical cleft through the right side of the whole face and forehead in the mid-orbital line. There are two knife-cuts below the left eye. A vertical crack extends from the gash above the left ear to a large hole 0 m. 144 mill. by 0 m. 09 cent. in the vertex of the skull. The left hip-bone was broken. All the ribs were broken in the mid-axillary line and the front of the chest-wall lost.

The right scapula and the upper part of the humerus were smashed off (not cut) in their bandages. The elbow was hacked through with an axe, leaving the head of the radius and part of the olecranon attached to the humerus. The wrist was chopped through with an axe in an oblique direction. The right hand is missing ; but the right hands of two other mummies were found amongst the wrappings. The left scapula and outer half of the clavicle are still attached to the body. The humerus was torn off at the shoulder joint and the middle of the shaft of the humerus (still in its wrappings) was broken across. The elbow was hacked through with an axe leaving the upper ends of the radius and ulna attached to the humerus. The left hand, fingers and wrist exhibit numerous axe-cuts. The cranial cavity had been packed with pieces of linen and resinous paste. The membranes of the brain were preserved. The nasal fossæ were packed with linen as far back as the pharynx.

Ramesses VI was apparently middle-aged—probably older than Ramesses V, but younger than Ramesses IV. His body was embalmed in the same manner as those of his two predecessors. No hair (excepting the eyelashes) is visible upon the face to the naked eye; but with a lens closely shaven hair of the beard and moustache can be detected. The part of the scalp of the forehead that is visible is bald; but on the scalp elsewhere short hairs (about 1 millimetre long) are present. The face, including the eyes and forehead, was thickly plastered with resinous paste. The ears were pierced. The teeth are only slightly worn.

Ramesses VI is the last of the Ramesside kings whose bodies have been found. Perhaps the others were too much smashed by ancient robbers to be reparable by the restoring priests, perhaps they still lie hidden somewhere in the Valley of the Kings. All their tombs are known save one, and possibly this may yet be found and yield up its secret. (See Appendix II.)

CHAPTER VII

MUMMIFICATION IN THE XXIst DYNASTY

THE XXIst Dynasty was a period in which the whole technique of the embalmer's art underwent the most curious and profound modifications. It must be remembered that, during the reign of the priest-king Hrihor and his immediate successors, great activity was displayed in restoring the plundered remains of the kings of the three preceding dynasties whose mummies we have dealt with in the foregoing chapter. The story of the great and daring robberies which were perpetrated in the Royal Necropolis during the XXth Dynasty is given at length in Appendix I, together with some account of the papyri which have preserved to us the judicial proceedings taken against the malefactors. When the first great find of royal mummies was made at Deir-el-Bahari in 1881, a considerable number of the coffins bore hieratic inscriptions written in ink, recording the restoration of each respective mummy, or the steps taken to preserve it from desecration by removing it to another tomb.[1] The robbers in their search for treasure had hacked away the bandages and damaged the bodies, and the pious restorers had to set about rebandaging these battered remains. In the course of doing so they must have been struck by the failure of the embalmer's art to

---

[1] Facsimiles of these hieratic *graffiti* with transliterations and translations will be found in Maspero's *Momies Royales*, and translations alone in Breasted, *Ancient Records*, vol. iv.

preserve the life-like appearance of their predecessors. It seems most probable that it was the contemplation of the shrunken and distorted forms of many of these mummies that impressed on the embalmers of the XXIst Dynasty the imperfections of their craft. We do know, at least, that immediately after the striking object-lesson afforded by the handling of these mummies of the XVIIIth, XIXth and XXth Dynasties, the embalmers of the XXIst Dynasty set to work to devise some means of restoring to the mummy the fulness of limb and features that it had possessed during life but had lost during the process of embalming.

There were two possible ways of restoring the shape of the mummy : (1) by external application of materials to its surface, or (2) by packing them underneath the skin. In other words, the embalmer had the option of building up the shape of the wrapped mummy or of the body itself. The former method had been tried in the Pyramid Age (see above, p. 75) and long afterwards had some vogue in Græco-Roman times. The second method had indeed been tried in the case of the mummy of Amenophis III, but seems to have been immediately abandoned until the embalmers of the XXIst Dynasty revived it. We know that it was not attempted during the time of the XIXth and XXth Dynasties. If the mummy of Tutankhamen is examined, perhaps it will provide us with decisive information as to whether the practice of packing mummies was one of the reforms associated with Aten worship and was discarded when the heresy was overthrown.

Examination of mummies of the XXIst Dynasty suggests that the motive of the embalmers was not merely to preserve the body and restore its life-like form, but also to convert it into the portrait statue and to identify this representation as completely as possible with the individuality of the deceased. Thus the restored body was painted like a statue and every organ that had been removed by the embalmers was restored to it to complete its integrity. Not only so, but any defects were repaired and the mummy made as presentable as possible. That it was the intention to transform it into a statue is confirmed by the fact that the use of portraits made of wood or stone seems to have fallen into abeyance at the time when this new device in embalming was introduced.

This inference is not affected by the fact that in later times, under other circumstances, the custom of making statues and portraits was revived in a somewhat modified form.

Happily we have abundant material upon which to found a study of the technical processes of this period. Nine royal, and over forty priestly, mummies of the XXIst Dynasty alone have been subjected to minute scientific examination and the results recorded.[1]

The earliest royal mummy of this period is that of Queen Nozme (Fig. 30), the wife of Hrihor, the first king of the XXIst Dynasty at Thebes. It is of peculiar interest to note that the first method of packing is employed in the case of her mummy, whilst in all her successors the second method was resorted to. There are certain indications that suggest a possible reason for the adoption of the much more difficult operation of stuffing the body in preference to the simpler procedure of padding. For many details of the technique of embalming that make their appearance for the first time in these XXIst Dynasty mummies go to prove what was suggested above—namely, that the idea of the

---

[1] See Elliot Smith : *The Royal Mummies*, pp. 94–111, and *Mémoires de l'Inst. Egypt.*, t. v, 1906. Minute descriptions, with anatomical details of individual mummies, were also contributed to the *Annales du Service*, 1903, pp. 13–17 ; 1906, pp. 1–28, with 9 plates, etc.

FIG. 43.—ARM OF AN EARLY CHRISTIAN BODY WITH A CROSS TIED TO IT

FIG. 44.—WOODEN COFFIN OF THE MIDDLE EMPIRE, SHOWING THE MYSTIC EYES. (XIIth DYNASTY)

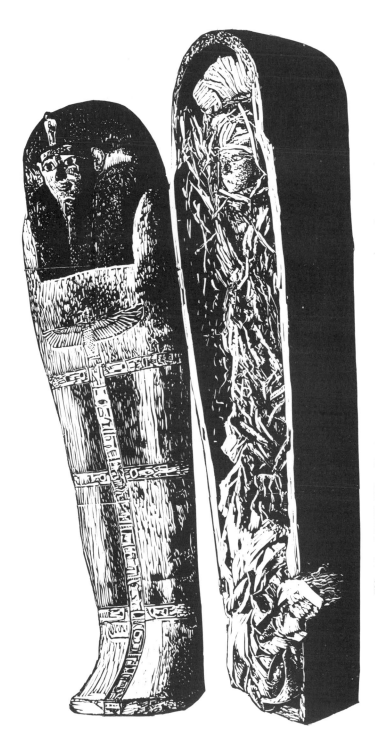

FIG. 45.—COFFIN AND MUMMY OF THE PHARAOH AMENOPHIS I (XVIIIth DYNASTY)

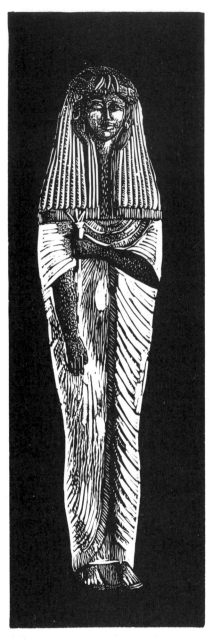

FIG. 46.—" CIVIL-DRESS " COFFIN
(xxth DYNASTY)

Now in the Berlin Museum

embalmers was to make the body not only as life-like, but also as complete, as possible, so that it might represent the deceased and take the place both of his actual remains and of the funerary statue which was placed in his tomb in earlier times.

The whole body was painted with red or yellow ochre and gum, just as the statues used to be treated ; artificial eyes were inserted ; the cheeks and neck were filled out with stuffing ; the forms of the trunk and limbs were restored ; and the viscera, which it had been customary to set apart in the four canopic jars, were now restored to the body so as to make it whole and complete. That this idea of making the body itself complete determined the choice between " external " and " internal " padding in favour of the latter, is suggested by the fact that the practice of replacing the viscera and inserting artificial eyes was already coming into vogue in the XXth Dynasty,[1] before any attempt was made to remedy the defects of its external form.

The mummy of Queen Nozme, then, belongs to the transition period, when the embalmers were attempting to restore the form of the wrapped mummy. There is no trace of any packing *within* the limbs or neck, but the face is stuffed through the mouth, and quantities of sawdust kept in position with resin-soaked bandages are applied to the abdomen, legs, buttocks and other parts of the body. The embalming-wound has no definite plate to cover it, but a lump of wax was plugged into the orifice. The eye-brows, instead of being emphasised by paint, were provided with

---

[1] As for instance in the Mummies of Ramesses IV and V (Elliot Smith : *Royal Mummies*, pp. 87–92), and the " Leeds Mummy " embalmed in the reign of Ramesses XI (W. Osburn : *Account of an Egyptian Mummy presented to the Museum of the Leeds Literary and Philosophical Society*, Leeds, 1828).

wisps of human hair, placed longitudinally and gummed on. Artificial eyes were inserted under the eyelids. These eyes, made of black and white stone, are the earliest instance of an attempt to represent the pupil in artificial eyes of a mummy, although in statues such eyes had been in use for many centuries.

The face was tightly packed with sawdust, so that the cheeks are filled out and the face assumes an almost circular shape. The body-cavity was packed through the embalming-wound with sawdust, but no trace of the viscera could be found. The hands were not placed in front of the abdomen, but vertically alongside the hips—a custom which became general in royal mummies of the XXIst Dynasty, both in men and women, as had been the practice at the commencement of the XVIIIth Dynasty. The mummies of the priests and priestesses of Amen, on the contrary, of the same dynasty, usually had the hands placed so as to conceal the pudenda.[1] On the wrists several bead bracelets were found.[2]

In the mummy of Queen Makerē a much more elaborate technique is manifested.[3] In spite of the damage done by the plunderers, it is still possible to discern that every part of the body had been internally packed and moulded into the shape of the Queen when alive, and wrapped in linen of marvellously fine texture. The face was painted with a mixture of yellow ochre and gum, which has caused the muslin sheet placed upon it to adhere.

The embalmer had packed the neck with a quantity of

---

[1] The mummy of a priestess of Amen of this period, for example, figured in the *Annales du Service*, t. iv, 1906, Pl. VII, had the hands so placed.

[2] For technical description of this mummy see *Royal Mummies*, pp. 94–8.

[3] Prof. Naville, who published the papyrus of this queen (*Papyrus Funeraires de la XXIe Dynastie*, vol. i), holds that the name should be Kamara by analogy with the cuneiform transcription of the prenomen of Amenophis III.

fat (possibly butter) mixed with soda, which had so filled out the skin as to give it the plump appearance of a living body, in great contrast to the shrunken and emaciated aspect of the necks of earlier mummies. This packing was inserted by putting the hand into the embalming-wound and passing it up through the thoracic region. The body-cavity was filled with sawdust. The embalmers separated the skin from the underlying muscular tissues in the anterior margin of the embalming-wound, and into the space thus formed the operator placed his hand and forced it up under the skin in front of the chest, filling the cavity thus formed with coarse linen. No attempt had been made to pack the breasts, but the rest of the bust was moulded upon this foundation of linen packing. The breasts in this mummy were enormously enlarged, as the Queen was lactating, and the mummy of her infant was buried in the same coffin with her.[1] The Queen therefore died at or soon after childbirth.

This mummy exemplifies in several particulars the elaborate methods of packing employed at this period, and it will be convenient to describe it in more general terms. The whole operation was one of great complexity and difficulty. Through the wound made in the left flank (Fig. 31, X) for the purpose of removing the viscera, the embalmer introduced his hand and arm and pushed it up through the body-cavity along the line Z, to stuff the neck (T) with linen, mud, butter, or some other material, a plug of linen then being inserted at W to retain the stuffing. The hand, or some instrument, was then introduced in turn from the body-cavity into each thigh (Y), and in this way stuffing was then pushed (U) into the whole leg as far as the ankle.

---

[1] Unfortunately it has not been possible to get a radiograph of this baby. When this has been done its age and sex can be determined.

Sometimes additional incisions were made in the skin of the foot (*i* and *e*), and, more rarely, also in the region of the ankle (*d*) and knee (*c*) to permit more efficient packing of these parts of the limb. When the neck and legs were packed, the preserved viscera, wrapped in linen, were restored to the body-cavity (Fig. 39). The skin was then separated from the muscles of the body-wall in both lips of the embalming-incision (Fig. 31, X) in the left flank, and packing material was introduced to restore the form of the bust (S), as well as the back (R and Q). Where special difficulties were encountered, additional incisions were made

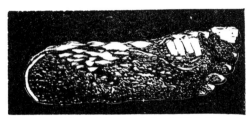

Foot of a Priest of Amen of the XXIst Dynasty
to show semi-lunar incision at the heel made for
packing the sole

(*f*, *g* and *h*). The shoulders and arms were packed through special incisions (*a*) in the shoulder (Fig. 32), while the cheeks were packed through the mouth.[1]

The mummy of Queen Henttaui (Fig. 33) was treated in this manner, but the embalmers had rather over-packed the body. An exceptionally large quantity of cheese-like material was packed into the mouth, and with the deliquescence of the salts mixed with the fat, the stretched skin of the cheeks had burst open on each side, from the outer angle of the eye downwards to the chin.[2]

---

[1] For a fuller account of the technical processes of " packing " with anatomical details, see Elliot Smith: *Mémoires d'Institut Égyptien*, t. v, fasc. i, pp. 19–28.   [2] *Royal Mummies*, Pls. LXXV and LXXVI.

THE XXIst DYNASTY

Although the plunderers had ransacked this mummy, an object of great value had escaped them. Amongst the disordered wrappings the end of a string was found, and on tracing this, it was found to be attached to a magnificent gold plate which had covered the embalming-wound and had originally been tied round the waist. This plate is the finest example yet found, and its weight is estimated as that of eighty sovereigns. It is unique in having not only the customary magical eye, but figures of the four children of Horus, who guarded the viscera (see below, p. 145) with their names and the titles and cartouches of the Queen.[1]

As in the case of most of the queens, the natural hair is supplemented by an artificial wig. The face was painted yellow, the cheeks and lips red and the eyebrows black. The body-cavity contained amongst the sawdust with which it was packed remains of the viscera which had been replaced and of the wax figures of the guardian genii placed there with them (see below, p. 146). The embalming-wound was plugged with a large mass of resinous paste, which had forced its lips apart, and on its outer surface was a plate of wax. This mummy displayed a curious treatment of the perineum, the only instance of its kind so far discovered. When the embalmers had removed the viscera, the pelvic cavity was cleared completely of its contents and a plug of linen was applied to the perineum and secured in position by means of a thick string, which was passed through the pelvis and out through the embalming-wound, down to the perineum again.

In the mummy of Masahirti, who was the son of the priest-king Pinozem I, we have the same general treatment applied to the body of a man, the mummies described above

---

[1] *Op. cit.* p. 102, and Pl. LXXVI, fig. 2.

all being of women. The adhesion of the innermost bandages to the skin, the whole being strongly impregnated with resin, has formed a hard carapace, as was the case in the above described mummies. The tendency to over-pack the face is very manifest in this mummy, producing a grotesque orang-outan-like appearance. The face was painted with red ochre, red being the colour for men and yellow for women, on statues and wall-paintings from the earliest times. As was customary in male mummies of this dynasty, the whole body was coloured with ochre and gum-paint. The hands were placed in front of the pubic region, but, owing to the great corpulency of the body, they do not reach far enough to conceal the pudenda as was intended. This mummy has the embalming-wound in the site which was usual in the late XVIIIth Dynasty, namely, parallel to Poupart's ligament, instead of in the contemporary position, high up above the level of the iliac spine. This exception to the rule, like others that have been examined, had a reason for it, which in this instance was the extreme corpulence of the subject.[1]

The mummy of this man's mother, Queen Isiemkheb, was so perfect and its bandages so undisturbed that it has not been unrolled, but it would be interesting to obtain an X-ray photograph of it.[2] The next royal mummy of the series, that of Pinozem II, conforms in every way to the custom of his time, the body-cavity being packed with sawdust and with linen parcels contained the separately embalmed viscera.[3]

In the mummies of the princesses Nesikhons (Fig. 34) and Nesitanebasher (Fig. 35) we come to two of the finest specimens of the embalmer's art in the XXIst Dynasty. The packing and moulding of the limbs and trunk have been

[1] *Royal Mummies*, p. 106 and Pl. LXXIX.
[2] *Op. cit.* Pl. LXXX.   [3] *Op. cit.* p. 107, Pl. LXXXI.

most skilfully accomplished, and the fault of over-packing and distending the face has not been repeated. In spite of the skill the craftsmen had acquired in the very difficult operation of packing, it is curious that they did not make any attempt to model the bust, for the breasts are flattened and pressed against the body-wall. The arms were fully extended, in the first case the palms were turned inwards on the outer surface of the thighs, in the second were placed upon the front of the thighs.

In the large series of mummies (forty-four) of priests and priestesses of Amen of this dynasty, which were examined in 1904, many interesting features were found, which show the great skill of the embalmers of the period. For instance, they made a successful mummy of a man with the extreme deformation of the spine which results from Pott's disease.[1] In another case the embalming-wound, instead of being left gaping, as was the usual custom, was neatly sewed up with string (Fig. 36). In the case of an extremely emaciated old woman, whose general condition indicated that she had long been bedridden, a curious state of affairs was revealed. Large open ante-mortem wounds, probably bed-sores, were found on the back between the shoulders and upon the buttocks. These had been made use of for the purpose of packing the back, and then neatly patched with square pieces of thin leather, perhaps gazelle-skin. These patches were sewn on to the healthy skin beyond the affected region, and the sutures concealed by strips of linen smeared with resin. A large abscess in the perineal area had been closed and sewn up with string, and an ulcer on one of the legs had been covered up by a patch of resin-soaked linen (Fig. 37).

---

[1] Published by Elliot Smith and Ruffer in Part III of *Zur historischen Biologie der Krankheitserreger*, 1910, and see, below, p. 156.

EGYPTIAN MUMMIES

The heart was always carefully left *in situ* (except when accidentally severed by unskilful manipulation) attached to its great blood-vessels (Fig. 38), and the other viscera were wrapped into four separate parcels, each with a wax figure of its appropriate guardian genius, and returned to the body-cavity (Fig. 39). The viscera will be more fully dealt with in Chapter IX under the heading of Canopic Jars.

It has been stated above that it was the custom in the XXIst Dynasty to paint the body red. In a few cases the body was not so painted, but a red linen shroud was applied to the mummy in such cases. In course of time it became usual to dye the outer shroud red, and in Ptolemaic times the cartonnage decorations were sewn on to this red background. (See Frontispiece.)

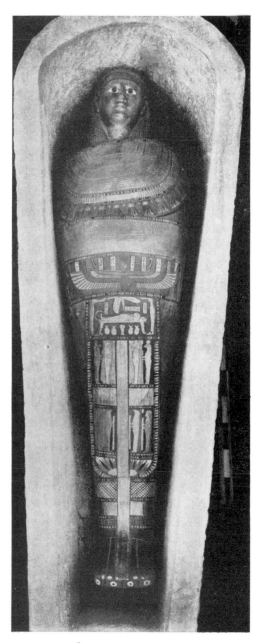

FIG. 47.—A RISHI-COFFIN
DISCOVERED AT THEBES
BY THE METROPOLITAN
MUSEUM EXPEDITION OF
NEW YORK

FIG. 48.—PTOLEMAIC MUMMY IN
CARTONNAGE CASING

FIG. 49.—A SET OF CANOPIC JARS

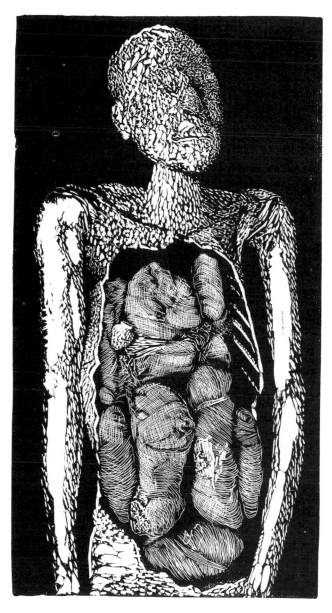

FIG. 50.—MUMMY OF THE XXISt DYNASTY WITH THE
VISCERA WRAPPED IN LINEN PARCELS AND REPLACED
IN THE BODY

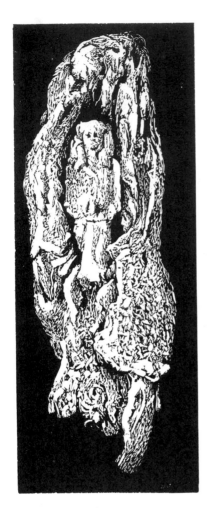

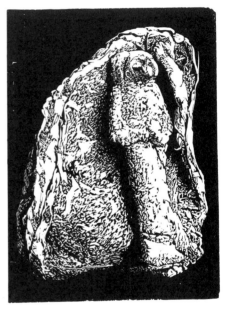

FIG. 51.—LIVER FROM A
XXIst DYNASTY MUMMY, WITH
HUMAN-HEADED WAX FIGURE

FIG. 52.—LUNG FROM A XXIst DYNASTY
MUMMY, WITH THE APE-HEADED
WAX FIGURE

CHAPTER VIII

MUMMIFICATION FROM THE XXIIND DYNASTY TO THE DECLINE

THE curious innovations in the technical processes of embalming described in the last chapter were maintained throughout the XXIInd Dynasty, but thereafter the art rapidly declined. The embalmers of the XXIst Dynasty aimed at making the body as perfect and as complete as possible, but as time went on less and less attention was paid to the body and more and more to the external wrappings. In other words, so long as the mummy displayed a presentable exterior it seemed to matter little to the embalmer how careless and slipshod was his work upon the corpse concealed beneath the carefully wrought external coverings.

Although the great museums of the world contain many mummies of the later periods, for the most part they are merely curios devoid of any scientific interest, as few of them have been unrolled or even photographed by X-rays. Our information from Egypt itself is so meagre, that for later periods we have to rely very largely upon the data afforded by the examination of a very large series of mummies from Nubia, discovered and examined during the archæological survey of that country.[1]

---

[1] See the *Bulletins* and *Reports* of the Archæological Survey of Nubia, particularly vol. ii of the Report for the season 1907–8. This volume deals exhaustively with the human remains.

121

EGYPTIAN MUMMIES

In the Cairo Museum is a good specimen of the mummy of a man who was embalmed during the reign of Sheshonk I, and which was found with the Royal Mummies at Dier-el-Bahari in 1881.[1] The general style of mummification conforms to the customs of the XXIst Dynasty. The hands are extended in front of the pubis, the body-cavity is packed with dried lichen (*Parmelia furfuracea*) and the viscera, wrapped in linen parcels, are replaced in the body. The practice of stuffing has been carried out, but very imperfectly, and no attempt has been made to pack some parts of the body, and we can see the beginning of the decline, which soon led to the entire abandonment of the packing process. The finger-nails were fixed on to the digits with rings of gold wire. On the left arm of this mummy some interesting amulets were found. The brain was removed through the right nostril.

We know of no accurate descriptions of any mummies between this period and the Persian occupation of Egypt, nor have we had facilities for examining any specimens. Two mummies of the Persian period were examined by the late Sir Armand Ruffer. In his report [2] no archæological details are given, nor is it stated where the mummies were found, but they exhibit a striking deterioration in technique. A piece of stick had been thrust up the body through the perineum by the embalmer to consolidate the carelessly made mummy. The body had been emptied of its contents through the usual embalming-wound, but the cavity was not packed tightly, only a few pieces of linen having been put in. The embalming-wound was closed with a plug of

---

[1] This is Maspero's " Zodphtahefônkh " or " Zadptahefonkhou," *Momies Royales*, p. 572 ; *Guide du Visiteur*, fourth ed., p. 401. Elliot Smith: *The Royal Mummies*, pp. 112–114, and Pls. LXXXIX–XCII.

[2] *Bulletin de la Soc. Arch. d'Alexandrie*, No. 14, 1912.

linen. The brain had been removed through a perforation in the ethmoid bone, and parts of the membranes remained in the skull, but no artificial filling had been introduced. The face showed a condition similar to facial paralysis, but it cannot be said with certainty whether this is a pathological condition or merely a distortion due to careless embalming. The other mummy was in even worse condition. It was, when wrapped up, of the usual mummy shape, but on unrolling it, it turned out to be practically nothing more than a skull and the leg bones, the body being made up of a kind of crate of palm-fibres into which the bones of the rest of the skeleton had been flung higgledy-piggledy.

For the Ptolemaic period we have an abundance of material from Nubia.[1] The conclusions to be drawn from this mass of data are in general agreement with what we know of embalming practices in Egypt itself, where the Ptolemaic period is especially distinguished by the extraordinary elaboration of the geometrical patterns made in applying the superficial bandages to the mummy, and by the perfection of the cartonnage decorations which were placed upon the mummies. At this period less and less attention was being paid to the care of the body itself. Whilst there are some specimens from Nubia which show great care and attention on behalf of the embalmer (see Fig. 40), the great majority of them are makeshifts of the most careless description.

The mummies of the Ptolemaic period are uniformally dark in colour, their surface is hard and often shining from the abundance of resinous matter or bitumen employed. This was usually applied direct to the skin, and has permeated the lowest layers of bandage which become corroded and

---

[1] *Report on the Human Remains*, pp. 194 ff.

solidified. As in mummies of earlier periods, the epidermis is nearly always absent owing to maceration, and the same methods as of old are employed to affix the nails. The shed epidermis was often collected and wrapped in a linen package, and placed inside the body-cavity or upon the perineum. In a few cases the viscera were wrapped up and returned to the body, as was the custom in Egypt in the XXIst Dynasty. The hair, if not matted in resinous material, was usually intact, and in the case of women long and flowing. The eyes and mouth were seldom closed. Linen, or mud-filling, was generally employed for packing these cavities, though resin and wax are occasionally found. In one case the mouth of a woman was completely filled with one of her own lumbar vertebræ wrapped in linen. The nostrils were usually plugged with resin or wax, and in some cases the orbits were stuffed with linen or mud in front of the shrunken eyes.

In most cases the brain was removed by the usual passage forced through the ethmoid bone. In such cases the skull is either left empty or filled with resin. In a good number of cases no attempt had been made to remove the brain. The resinous material nearly always lay at the back of the skull and was not nearly sufficient in quantity to fill the whole cavity. As there is no trace of resin in the nose, it must have been poured through a funnel in a molten condition, as the body lay on its back. In some cases the head had been completely separated from the trunk, presumably as the result of decomposition due to faulty treatment, and refixed by passing a stick through the body into the foramen magnum (see Fig. 41). In such cases the resinous matter lay in the vertex, and must have been poured in through the foramen when the skull was detached and inverted ; as no perforation had been made in the ethmoid bone.

XXIIND DYNASTY TO THE DECLINE

With regard to the body-cavity, a relatively small number of bodies, and those mostly of children, had no incision, and the viscera remained *in situ*. In one case, although there was no embalming-wound, the whole of the viscera had been removed ; this could only have been done through the anus, and corresponds to the " second method " of Herodotus (see p. 58), although the brain had been removed by the nasal route which characterises his " most expensive method." Where the viscera had been removed, some variation in treatment may be observed. In some cases the thorax was intact and the diaphragm uninjured ; in other cases the diaphragm had been perforated or completely excised and the whole of the chest and abdomen emptied. The heart was generally left *in situ*, except when careless manipulation had dragged it out along with the other thoracic viscera. As already mentioned, the viscera were sometimes made into packages and put into the body-cavity, but in so doing no care was taken to replace them in their correct anatomical position. The parcels are often packed in without any regard to order, which is quite arbitrary and varies in almost every case. When the viscera were not returned to the body, the cavity was usually filled with balls of resin-soaked linen, but occasionally mud, broken pottery and all kinds of household refuse were used for the purpose. In other cases the whole cavity was filled with molten resin or bitumen, which has permeated every tissue and has even found its way into the structure of the bones.[1]

It may be observed that there is abundant evidence that some of the bodies were in an advanced stage of decomposition when treated by the embalmers, and this condition in nearly every case applied to women. This may lend some

[1] Other technical details concerning the measures taken for plugging the natural orifices will be found in the *Report of the Archæological Survey of Nubia.*

support to the statement of Herodotus concerning tendencies towards necrophilia. In *Euterpe*, Bk. II, c. lxxxix, Herodotus says : " But the wives of considerable persons, when they die, they do not immediately deliver to be embalmed, nor such women as are very beautiful and of celebrity, but when they have been dead three or four days they deliver them to the embalmers ; and they do this for the following reason, that the embalmers may not abuse the bodies of such women ; for they say that one man was detected in abusing a body that was fresh, and that a fellow-workman informed against him." [1] It is very evident that, by the time the embalmers came to pour the molten bitumen into the body, it was already the host of a vast number of maggots and beetles. These insects are seen very commonly, caught in the invading stream of bitumen, and killed and preserved as they were engaged in the process of devouring the body (see Fig. 42).

In addition to the invasion of insects and the partial decomposition of the body, there must have been some period in the process of embalming at which some of the bodies became so decomposed as partly to disintegrate. The evidence for this statement lies in the finding of a great number of mummies, parts of which are in a state of such utter confusion that it is clear that the body must have fallen to pieces during the process of embalming. This state of affairs must not be confounded with the rewrapping and restoring of bodies plundered by robbers, as was the case, for instance, in the mummy of Ramesses VI (see above, p. 106). It is clearly due to grossly careless manipulation. In the case of one of the Nubian mummies, the cartonnage and outer wrappings were quite undisturbed, but the perished parts of the body had been made good by stuffing in bits of

---

[1] Carey's translation, ed. Bohn, 1872, p. 127.

broken pottery. In another case, where the outer wrappings were very carefully applied, the " body " was a collection of bones made up of parts of no less than three individuals. The mummy, exteriorly, was that of a child, but when opened it was found to have the skull of an adult woman, an artificial neck, some of the lumbar vertebræ, a complete set of ribs, but only one side of the pelvis. There was a female femur and tibia but articulated to the fibula of a large muscular man. The other leg had a male femur, put upside down, but articulated to it was another male fibula from a different skeleton. A number of similar cases were found and are described in the Nubian report already cited (pp. 213–215).[1] Several mummies had false hands, their own hands having decomposed, and the carpal bones having been thrown into the body-cavity. Many of these " faked " mummies were strengthened by sticks, or the mid-ribs of palm leaves. In several cases the stick carried all the weight and was thrust through the perineum upwards, and, projecting through the neck, transfixed the skull by the foramen magnum. In one case the head was affixed to the trunk and the supporting stick by an elaborate lacing of bandages passing through the angles of the mouth and over the ears. (Fig. 41.) [2]

In the Roman period mummification still further deteriorated. The bodies so far examined seem to prove that they were simply treated with hot bitumen, or a mixture of resin and pitch. They are so thickly coated with this material that it is impossible to say whether evisceration or the removal of the brain was practised. The embalmer's sole object seems to have been a summary treatment of the body to prevent decay in order to leave him free to develop the greater elaboration of the external wrappings, which

---

[1] Several " false mummies " were found at Dier-el-Bahari in 1881.
[2] See additional note, p. 132.

reaches its greatest development in the Roman period when the external mummy was lavishly bedecked and a painted portrait of the deceased affixed to the head. Coffins and wrappings are separately dealt with in a later chapter, so no further reference will be made to them here.[1]

Among the collection of mummies sent by the late Sir Gaston Maspero to the Cairo School of Medicine in 1904 were the remains of two young women that call for special notice. One of them was a mummy, possibly of late Ptolemaic or early Roman date, to the surface of which large masses of bandages and resinous paste had been applied and moulded into a form recalling the best of the statuettes of Aphrodite found in Egypt. The modelling was carried out with great skill. A statue of stony hardness had been successfully shaped out of such unpromising materials as linen and resin applied to the mummified body of a young woman, which had been idealised and transformed into a model of pleasing aspect and grace. On the skilfully modelled breasts the nipples were represented by buttons of copper, and another disc of the same metal was fixed in the depression of the navel. So far as we are aware this mummy is unique. But it gives expression to the agelong aim of the embalmer, to preserve the life-like form of the dead.

The other body that deserves special notice revealed no certain evidence of embalming and nothing (apart from its linen shroud and wrappings) to indicate its age. No record had been preserved in the Cairo Museum of Antiquities as to its provenance. But the character of the linen and the absence of evidence distinctive of the earlier or later periods suggest that the young women, whose tragic story is revealed

---

[1] See Petrie : *Hawara, Biahmu and Arsinöe*, ch. iii.

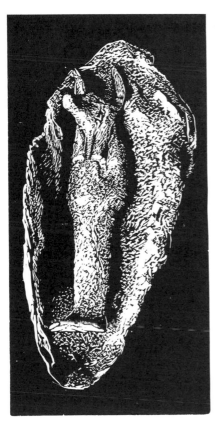 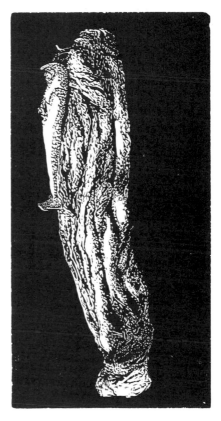

FIG. 53.—STOMACH OF A XXIst DYNASTY
MUMMY, WITH THE JACKAL-HEADED
WAX FIGURE

FIG. 54.—SMALL INTESTINES OF A
MUMMMY (XXIst DYNASTY) WITH
THE FALCON-HEADED WAX FIGURE

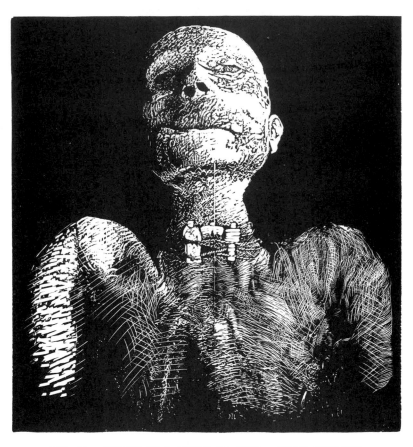

FIG. 55.—MUMMY OF A PRIEST OF AMEN. (XXISt DYNASTY)
Showing the amulets tied round the neck

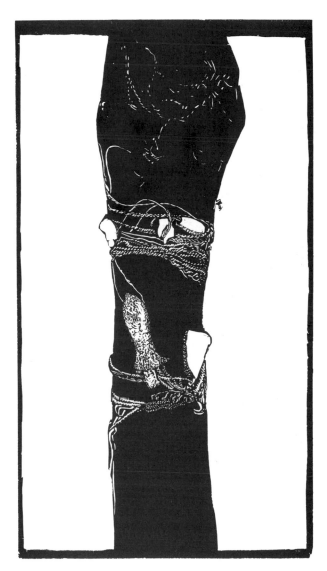

FIG. 56.—ARM FROM MUMMY

Showing the amulets tied on with string

FIG. 57.—ARM AND PART OF THE BODY OF A MUMMY
Showing amulets and the plate covering the embalming-wound

by the bones within the shroud, lived during the years immediately before the Persian conquest of Egypt.

After one of us had unwrapped all the mummies sent to the Cairo Medical School in 1904, excepting one of mean appearance that seemed to lack any particular interest, the late Sir Alexander Simpson, who had then recently retired from the Professorship in Midwifery in the University of Edinburgh, visited the Cairo School and expressed the desire to see the unwrapping of a mummy. While the only unwrapped mummy in the collection was being prepared, Sir Alexander was informed, in answer to his enquiries, that no case of pregnancy had ever been found in a mummy because the embalmer removed all the viscera excepting the heart and the kidneys. Yet by a very remarkable coincidence the body actually being unwrapped when this conversation took place proved to be that of a young woman of sixteen years of age in the sixth month of pregnancy. There was, however, no certain evidence of mummification, as nothing but the bones were found within the wrappings. Immediately before her death this girl had had both her forearms broken and had been killed by a blow on the head which had fractured her skull. Perhaps in these facts we have the record of an incident for which many parallels might be found in modern Egypt. For it is no uncommon occurrence when the relatives discover that a girl has committed an indiscretion—the results of which in the case we are considering became apparent at the sixth month of pregnancy—to set on her with sticks and kill her. From the injuries revealed in her bones it is clear that she put up one hand after the other to fend the blow and had both her wrists broken in turn. Then, when she was writhing upon the ground in her agony, she received the fatal blow upon her head. The body was probably prepared for burial in summary fashion, without the care that would have been bestowed upon her remains if she had not been disgraced. The body was neither eviscerated nor really embalmed.

Mummification lingered on in some parts of Egypt and Nubia long after the introduction of Christianity, but after it had been abandoned as such, measures were still taken for the preservation of the body. The Christian cemeteries in Nubia have supplied us with ample material for the study of the subject.[1] The body was not placed in a coffin of any kind, but often it was laid upon a board, which was roughly shaped to fit it. In one case a stout rope was found tied about the middle of a body passing under the board by which it had evidently been lowered into the grave. The change from Paganism to Christianity brought about a great difference in the treatment of the dead. There was no longer any necessity to make the mummy into a simulacrum or representative of the dead man, which had been the object of the embalmer from the Pyramid Age to Roman times, and all attempts to make a presentable exterior of the mummy for the after-use of the dead man's spirit or " Ka " were given up, for the ideas which promoted these attempts were foreign to the new beliefs. Yet the careful preparation of the body for burial was by no means neglected, and deliberate attempts were made to preserve it from decay. Doubtless the preparation of the body as practised by these early Christians was inspired or influenced by the account of the treatment of the dead body of Christ in St. John's Gospel (chap. xix), and in that of St. Luke (chap. xxiii).

The bodies discovered were superficially similar to mummies of older periods, that is to say they were wrapped in linen sheets with transverse tapes or bandages to hold the shroud in position. Within the winding-sheet the body was

---

[1] *Arch. Survey, Nubia, Report on the Human Remains*, pp. 215–220.

found usually dressed in clothes, which were generally well made and often very beautifully embroidered. The women usually wore a long white garment like a modern night-dress, and the men a short shirt or tunic and drawers, the latter being tied round the waist and ankles by draw-strings. Many of the women and children had bead neck-laces, but no jewellery was found on the men except a cross of wood or iron hung about the neck or attached to the arm (Fig. 43). Some of the bodies wore boots of goat skin, with the fur turned inwards, the outer surface of the leather being tanned and polished and sometimes embroidered with a cross. The body itself was usually in an excellent state of preservation, so that every detail of its gross anatomy, both external and internal, could be studied. The method of preservation used by these people did not involve opening the body and removing its contents, but was accomplished by spreading around the body large quantities of common salt and certain vegetable substances. These latter were evidently the " spices " of the Christian embalmer. Salt was lavishly used and appears as large, hollow, pyramidal crystals ; it was distributed all round the body within the clothes and winding-sheet.

The effect of this treatment has been to preserve the skin entire, and to render it soft and pliable. The hands were placed at the sides of the body, or over the pubes ; in the case of women they seem to have been deliberately arranged to conceal the pudenda. It was the custom to tie the big toes together in order to prevent the legs from falling apart, and the thumbs were often similarly tied. The excellent preservation of the bodies enables us to say definitely that the practice of circumcision had been at last abandoned. The internal organs are so perfectly preserved, that from the examination of the alimentary canal and rectum the nature of the food consumed can be determined.

EGYPTIAN MUMMIES

How long these customs were maintained it is impossible to state, but they certainly survived, more or less, for several centuries of the Christian era, and are the last phases of the distinctively Egyptian custom of embalming which held sway continuously for at least thirty centuries.

Additional Note to p. 127.

Herodotus, II, 90, says :—

Should any person, whether Egyptian or stranger, no matter which, be found to have been seized by a crocodile, or drowned in the river, to whatever city the body may be carried, the inhabitants are by law compelled to have the body embalmed, and having adorned it in the handsomest manner, to bury it in the sacred vaults.[1]

Commenting upon this curious passage, Professor Griffith makes the following interesting remarks :—[2]

The fate of most animals that were drowned was to be devoured by crocodiles, who, so to speak, completed the work begun by the river; moreover, crocodiles overpower their prey by suffocating it in the water. It is not improbable that some of the made-up mummies, human or animal, which contain only odd bones, are the remains of crocodiles' dinners, perhaps extracted from their stomachs. Herodotus' statement . . . may be suspected of inaccuracy in details.

---

[1] Carey's translation, ed. Bohn, p. 127.
[2] *Zeitschrift für äg. Sprache*, t. 46 (1909), p. 134.

CHAPTER IX

THE ACCESSORIES OF THE MUMMY

IN this chapter only those articles of funerary furniture are dealt with which have direct association with the mummy itself. The whole contents of an Egyptian tomb were intimately bound up with the funerary cult, but in this book it is not within our province to describe nor to interpret the funerary furniture as a whole, but only the coffins, cartonnages and wrappings in which the mummy was enclosed, the canopic jars which are, in a sense, coffins for the viscera, and the amulets which were placed actually on the body or enclosed in the wrappings.

These objects are, as all are aware, themselves only a part of a consistent whole, but to enter into a discussion on the entire burial equipment would be, not merely out of place, but wellnigh impossible in the present state of our knowledge. The discoveries in the Tomb of Tutankhamen alone are daily bringing forward the necessity for new conceptions or a revision of old conceptions on these matters. Our function is merely to describe and not to interpret, but in the notes we have indicated the sources which must be tapped for fuller information.

COFFINS AND MUMMY-CASES

The oldest coffins, used merely as a medium to keep the body from contact with the earth, were large pottery dishes, or rude square boxes made of slabs of stone or planks of wood. The wooden coffin quickly became elaborated in proportion to the elaboration of the tomb itself. The coffin, in fact, became a small tomb within a tomb, and was decorated with architectural details reproducing those of the tomb. The inscriptions on the tomb wall were often duplicated on the inner walls of the coffin, and finally transferred entirely to the coffin.[1] The earliest wooden coffins are rare, and when discovered they are almost always in a fragile or decayed condition, and unfit for removal. Wooden coffins as old as the IInd Dynasty were found by Quibell at Saqqara (see Fig. 1). The Cairo Museum has specimens of the Vth and VIth Dynasties.[2] The decoration of these early coffins is a study by itself, and has been dealt with in many publications. The inscriptions comprise a long series of funerary spells now commonly called the *Coffin Texts* to distinguish them from the later texts which make up the *Book of the Dead* of the New Empire, and have been specially studied by Lacau, who has published a large series of them from coffins in the Cairo Museum to supplement those already published from other sources.[3] In addition to these texts, the coffins are adorned with a kind of frieze on which are depicted offerings to the dead and objects for his use in the next world.[4] The body was laid usually on its left side

---

[1] Cf. " The Tomb of Horhotpe," published by Maspero : *Miss. Arch.*, t. i, pp. 133 ff.

[2] Lacau : *Sarcophages anterieurs au Nouvel Empire*, t. ii, pp. 134, 135. Petrie : *Deshasheh*, Pl. XXIX.

[3] Lacau : *Textes religieux*, pt. i, Paris 1910 ; the same writer has published others in Quibell, *Excavations at Saqqara in* 1906–7, Cairo 1908, pp. 21–61. For the texts in general see Breasted : *Development of Religion and Thought*, London 1912, pp. 273 ff., where other collections of material are indicated. The texts are now being studied by M. Lacau, Dr. Gardiner and Prof. Breasted with a view to a complete edition of them.

[4] For these objects see especially Lacau : *Sarcophages*, and Jéquier : *Les Frises d'Objets des Sarcophages du Moyen Empire* (*Mem. Inst. Eg.*, t. xlvii, Cairo 1922). The plates of Lacau's book give numerous examples, and another series in colour will be found in Maspero's *Trois Années de Fouilles*, Cairo 1883. (*Mem. Miss. Arch.*, t. i).

in the coffin, and opposite to its face, two mystic eyes, symbolising the sun and moon, were painted on the outside of the coffin, to protect the dead man's head, just as they were traced upon many other objects for the same purpose (Fig. 44). These eyes, so placed on the coffin in the Middle Kingdom, went out of fashion in coffin decoration in later times, but occasionally reappeared, as for instance on the stone sarcophagus in which the mummy of Amenophis II to-day reposes in his tomb in the Valley of the Kings. The body was sometimes simply wrapped in bandages, but at least as early as the XIth Dynasty a cartonnage head-piece was put over the wrappings, so as to preserve the facial likeness of the dead man and perpetuate his identity (see below, p. 143). Sometimes more than one coffin was used, the inner coffin fitting closely within the outer. The inner coffin by the time of the early Middle Empire was often anthropoid in form, and represented the bandaged mummy in its cartonnage head-piece and linen shroud, usually with an elaborate pectoral ornament, and was a reduplication in wood of the actual mummy within, repeated in more durable materials. A good example of this arrangement can be seen in the mummy of Senebtisi, discovered at Lisht by the American Excavators.[1] The rectangular coffin, sometimes of wood and sometimes of stone, continued in use throughout the Middle Kingdom, with or without the anthropoid coffin within it.[2]

In the period intermediate between the Middle and New Empires a new fashion was introduced. The rectangular

---

[1] Fully described and figured in Winlock and Mace : *The Tomb of Senebtisi*, New York.

[2] See Lacau : *op. cit.* Garstang : *Burial Customs* (XIIth Dynasty), London 1907. Naville : *The Eleventh Dynasty Temple of Deir-el-Bahari*, pts. i–ii, London 1907–10. A series of these coffins is to be seen in the first Egyptian Room at the British Museum.

coffin was discontinued and a new form of anthropoid coffin took its place. In these the painted eyes were discontinued and the mummy was laid flat on its back. These coffins, called *rishi*-coffins, were made of wood, and represented the mummy with its face uncovered, and usually bedecked in a stiff angular head-dress, the body being entirely enfolded in a pair of wings (the wings of the protecting goddess Isis). These coffins were often covered in gold-leaf and have consequently been despoiled by the natives, but a number of interesting specimens has survived.[1] King Seknenrē of the XVIIth Dynasty, the earliest of the royal mummies found at Deir-el-Bahari, was buried in a *rishi*-coffin. (Daressy : *Cercueils de Cachettes Royales*, Pls. I and II, and pp. 1–2. Cairo 1909.) See Fig. 47.

In the XVIIIth Dynasty styles became diversified. The simplest form of coffin represented the mummy with a heavy wig, wrapped in its shroud with bandages encircling the body at regular intervals and crossing a vertical bandage running from the chest to the feet. All this was represented by painting, either on plain wood or on wood covered with a thin coating of plaster. The background was coloured white. A good example of this type is the coffin of Amenophis I (Fig. 45, and cf. Daressy, *op. cit.* Pls. VI, VII). Even in coffins of this type the *rishi*-motive of wings sometimes reappears (coffin of Ray, Daressy, *op. cit.* Pl. V). A perfectly plain coffin without the transverse bands, depicting the mummy with wig and pectoral ornaments only, is common in the early XVIIIth Dynasty. (Daressy, *op. cit.* Pls. IX, XI). In the coffin of Queen Aahotpe II,[2] we meet with

[1] The British Museum has five specimens, the Louvre and Cairo Museums have others. One discovered by Petrie is shown in Petrie, *Qurneh*, Pl. XXIV, and a fine one discovered at Thebes is figured in the *New York Metropolitan Museum Bulletin*, 1917, p. 13.

[2] Queen Aahotpe I had a *rishi*-coffin, which is now at Cairo. Maspero : *Guide*, ed. iv, p. 413, and fig. 118 (Cairo 1915).

FIG. 58.—MUMMY OF A PRIESTESS OF THE XXIst DYNASTY

Note the amulets tied on the arms and the plate bearing the sacred eye symbol covering the embalming-wound

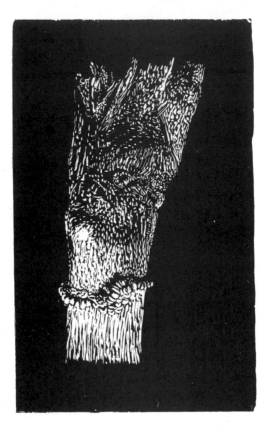

FIG 59.—ARM FROM A MUMMY, SHOWING
BEAD BRACELET

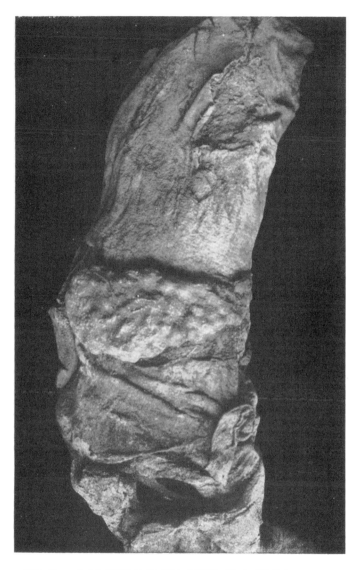

FIG. 60.—GALL-STONES IN THE LIVER OF A MUMMY OF THE
XXIst DYNASTY

FIG. 61.—MUMMY OF A PRIESTESS OF AMEN (XXIst DYNASTY) FROM WHICH THE GALL-STONES SHOWN IN FIG. 60 WERE TAKEN

quite a different type, which is somewhat similarly repeated in the case of Queen Nefretari. These coffins are made of wood and of linen pasteboard. The form represents the mummy wearing a heavy wig, the hands, which protrude from the bandages, grasp emblems of life. A single vertical band of inscription runs to the feet. The shoulders and arms are represented as covered in a woven shawl. On the head stand the two high plumes which are the head-dress of the god Amen. (Daressy, *op. cit.* Pls. III, VIII and IX.) A much greater elaboration in style now appears, and persisted, with infinite variations, until late times. The mummy is represented as bedecked with jewellery, and elaborate ear-rings, pectorals, and bracelets in multi-coloured paint, or worked in inlaid paste, make their appearance. The ground is still divided into compartments by what were originally simple bandages, and on these dividing lines prayers are inscribed, all the free space between which is filled with figures of protective deities. The custom of using two or more coffins one within the other still continues. The inside is usually painted white and covered with prayers or extracts from the *Book of the Dead,* and large figures of the goddess Isis on the bottom of the coffin who holds the mummy in her embrace, and of Nut (the sky-goddess) on the lid who spreads protectingly over the mummy in accordance with a very early funerary text.

Greater and greater elaboration of detail is employed, until the whole surface of the coffin is covered with inscriptions, emblems and scenes. The weighing of the heart, supplication before Osiris and other deities, and episodes from the passage of the sun through the twelve hours of the night, crowd closer and closer upon one another. It is unnecessary to indicate references to these coffins which develop in greater and greater elaboration throughout the XVIIIth, XIXth, XXth and XXIst Dynasties, as examples

EGYPTIAN MUMMIES

of them are innumerable in all museums. The general development can be conveniently seen by looking through the successive plates in Daressy's catalogue of the royal and priestly coffins in the Cairo Museum,[1] or by the inspection of the actual specimens in any museum.

It will be observed that all these devices are not merely decorative, but provide a magic garment of protection for the dead man, who is represented as a mummy bedecked in amulets and prayers for his welfare. Occasionally, however, the deceased appears not as a mummy, but as a living person in civil dress, in the condition, in fact, that the ceremony of *Opening the Mouth* (see p. 42) was intended to accomplish. Examples of this type are rare (until it became customary in Roman times), but a good specimen may be seen in the mummy-case of a woman discovered by Maspero in 1886 in the Theban Tomb of Sennozem of late XIXth or early XXth Dynasty date (Fig. 46). This beautiful coffin is now in the Berlin Museum, the contents of the tomb having unfortunately been dispersed without publication.

Reference may also be made to the fine series of anthropoid coffins of the priests of Mont, discovered by Mariette behind the temple at Deir-el-Bahari, and which are the subject of a special volume by H. Gauthier in the Cairo Museum Catalogue.[2]

Sarcophagi, although not used continuously, were never entirely discontinued. Massive stone sarcophagi were used for kings and nobles in the Old and Middle Empires. The stone sarcophagus of Cheops of the IVth Dynasty is still

---

[1] Daressy : *Cercueils des Cachettes Royales*, Cairo 1909, and Chassinat : *La Seconde Trouvaille de Deir-el-Bahari*, Cairo 1909, both of these volumes belong to the official series of Cairo Museum Catalogues. For a fine series of coffins of the latter end of the XVIIIth Dynasty see Quibell : *Tomb of Yuaa and Thuiu*, Cairo 1908, which belongs to the same series.

[2] *Cercueils anthropoïdes des Prêtres de Montou*, Cairo 1913.

MUMMY CASES

in his pyramid. That of Mycerinus was found in the third pyramid, but lost at sea. Fortunately a drawing of it survives.[1] In the Middle Kingdom stone sarcophagi were beautifully carved and painted, and those found by Naville at Deir-el-Bahari and now in the Cairo Museum are amongst the finest artistic productions of the period. Owing to their great weight many of these monuments are necessarily left *in situ* and not brought to European museums. Stone sarcophagi of the XVIIIth Dynasty are known by several examples found in the Royal Tombs at Thebes.[2]

The great alabaster sarcophagus of King Sety I of the XIXth Dynasty is a wonderful piece of workmanship. It is mummiform in shape, and is covered both inside and out with a complete copy of the *Book of Gates*, a mystical religious work which described the passage of the sun through the twelve hours of the night and the gates to each division through which he had to pass.[3] There are also extracts from the *Book of the Dead*. Large wooden sarcophagi, mounted on runners, which resemble in form the great hearses depicted in the funeral processions (see p. 40), were also sometimes used. For good examples those found in the Tomb of Yuaa cannot be surpassed.[4]

---

[1] Capart : *Egyptian Art*, London 1923, Pl. XIX.

[2] For sarcophagi of the Old Empire, cf. Maspero : *Ars Una*, Egypt 1921, figs. 42 and 43. For the Middle Empire, see Naville : *Eleventh Dynasty Temple* pt. i, Pls. XIX, XX, XXII, XXIII, etc. Maspero : *op. cit.* fig. 206. For the XVIIIth Dynasty, see Theodore M. Davis : *Tomb of Hatshopsitu,* and *Tomb of Thoutmôsis IV.* Maspero : *Struggle of the Nations*, p. 335, has a figure of the Sarcophagus of Ay, Tutankhamen's successor, and news has recently been announced of the discovery of the sarcophagus of Tutankhamen himself.

[3] This sarcophagus, now in Sir John Soane's Museum, was discovered by Belzoni in 1817 and brought by him to England. It was published by Bonomi and Sharpe : *The Alabaster Sarcophagus of Oimenepthah I,* London 1864. A general description of it, with illustrations, was published as an official museum handbook by Budge in 1908. See the same author's *Egyptian Heaven and Hell* (three vols.).

[4] Quibell : *Tomb of Yuaa and Thuiu,* Pls. I and VII.

EGYPTIAN MUMMIES

The coffins of the Saïte and Bubastite periods [1] are massive and elaborate but display a deterioration in art and workmanship which we cannot fail to recognise, although the massive stone sarcophagi which were used in this and later times are very fine both in sculpture and decoration, and are covered with texts and pictures from the *Book of Him who is in the Netherworld*.[2] In Greek times the deterioration is still more marked and an alien touch is felt.[3]

When we reach Roman times we find the Egyptian Symbolism less and less conspicuous in coffin-decoration. It was gradually passing out of use and was being misunderstood and its significance forgotten. The mummy-cases of this period were caricatures of their Pharaonic forerunners. Egyptian designs in a debased form survive, however, into the Christian period. Thus we have a coffin in the British Museum dated A.D. 110 displaying the goddess Nut, together with the twelve signs of the Zodiac.[4] Coffins made of papyrus-fibre of this period sometimes represent the dead entirely without funerary emblems and clad in civil dress.[5]

In Roman times the custom was introduced of discarding the cartonnage mask which had been in continuous use for many centuries, and of substituting therefor a wooden panel with an oil painting of the face of the deceased. The technique and artistic merit of these panels is wonderful, and a large series of them found by Petrie has been admirably reproduced in colour, and forms an important

---

[1] Moret : *Sarcophages de l'Époque Bubastite à l'Époque Saite*, Cairo 1913.
[2] *Guide to the Egyptian Galleries (Sculpture)*, British Museum 1909, pp. 224–248, and Pls. XXX–XXXIII.
[3] Maspero : *Sarcophages de l'Époques Persane et Ptolemaique*, Cairo 1908, and Edgar : *Græco-Egyptian Coffins*, (Cairo 1905).
[4] Brit. Mus., No. 6705, Third Egyptian Room.
[5] Brit. Mus., No. 29,585 : *Guide to First and Second Egyptian Rooms*, 1924, Pl. XXXIV. In this guide-book the style in use in late times is well illustrated and a comparison of the various types can be made.

contribution, not only to archæology, but to the history of art, and actual specimens may be seen, not only in museums, but in the National Gallery.[1]

From what has been said above as to the general deterioration in the manufacture of mummy-cases it must not be inferred that this is universal, although the general tendency. Fine specimens of all periods are known, but these are rather the exception than the rule.

BANDAGES.

Some reference was made to the bandaging of mummies in connexion with the Egyptian texts which relate to them (see pp. 46 ff.). The wrapping of the body in bandages was an essential part of the process of embalming, and from the time of the Ist Dynasty, in which the earliest instance of such wrapping occurs, it was continued until mummification was finally obsolete.

The wrappings consist of a number of linen bandages of various lengths and qualities, and of shrouds or winding-sheets. The actual method of applying them has been referred to from time to time in previous chapters in dealing with specific mummies, but in general terms it may be said that each limb, and in some cases each digit, was separately wrapped. The arms having been placed in position, either alongside the body or in various attitudes of flexion according to the period, the bandaging was continued over the whole, the trunk and limbs being bound up together in one parcel. At intervals a large sheet or shroud was wrapped round the body and tied at the head and foot, and the bandages reverted to. Several layers of alternate bandage and shroud often occur in one mummy.

---

[1] Petrie : *The Hawara Portfolio*, 1913 (24 subjects in colour) ; *Roman Portraits and Memphis IV*, 1911 (4 subjects in colour and others by photography). See also *Hawara, Biahmu and Arsinöe*, 1889, pp. 14–21 and 37–42.

EGYPTIAN MUMMIES

Amulets and other objects were placed in position as the wrapping proceeded, and sometimes a papyrus roll, containing the *Book of the Dead* or some other funerary composition, was placed between the legs and enveloped in the bandages.

The bandaging attained great elaboration in later periods, and the bandages were so arranged as to form a series of elaborate patterns.[1]

Occasionally, in addition to the linen bandages, shirts or garments were placed upon mummies. Thus when unrolling the mummy of Sety II several fragments of garments were found, and two perfectly intact shirts of very fine muslin. It is ever to be lamented that although these articles were immediately handed over to the conservator of the Cairo Museum, they mysteriously disappeared from the collection and could not be found when the official catalogue was prepared.[2] One of the royal mummies from Deir-el-Bahari was found enveloped in a sheep-skin. As far as we know, this instance is unique, but the mummy in question was altogether exceptional in its treatment and technique, and was supposed by Maspero to have been poisoned and buried alive.[3] In the early centuries of the Christian era, mummies were frequently clothed in garments made of fine linen and elaborately embroidered.

In the coffins of the Middle Kingdom folded sheets of linen were often laid over the mummy.

In spite of the great elaboration in the wrapping of mummies, our present available material is quite inadequate

---

[1] Of this, again, instances are so numerous in museums that only a few references need be given. The whole question is elaborately dealt with by Petrie : *Hawara*, ch. iii. A series of pictures will be found in the article on Mummies in *Wonders of the Past*.

[2] Smith Elliot : *The Royal Mummies*, pp. 74–5.

[3] *Les Momies Royales*, p. 548–551 and 778–782 ; *Struggle of the Nations*, p. 480.

BANDAGES

for a detailed study. Out of the hundreds of mummies in various museums, few have been unrolled. The royal mummies of Cairo had all been plundered and their wrappings reduced to mere torn bundles of rags. In a few cases the wrapping of mummies has been carefully recorded, but until we have many other such records of all periods for comparison it is wasted time to attempt to reduce our scanty information to order. The recorded instances of wrapping have already been cited (see p. 49, note 1).

Mummies are often found bearing leather or linen " braces " or straps, placed over the shoulders and crossed in front of the chest. Good examples of these were found in several of the royal mummies, and the " Leeds mummy " had " braces " bearing the cartouches of Ramesses XI.

CARTONNAGE.

Reference has been made above (p. 135) to the use of cartonnage masks. These are the development of the earlier methods employed to preserve the likeness of the dead man, whose features were concealed under the wrappings. We have already seen the attempt made to model the features on the resin-saturated bandages in the case of the Meidûm mummy (above, p. 75), and allusion has also been made to the use of substitute heads and death masks. The cartonnage mask gave rise, as we have already seen, to the anthropoid coffin, but was retained in conjunction with the latter, and developed. Instead of the mask and headdress of the Middle Kingdom mummies, a complete covering or envelope of cartonnage, laced up at the back, came into general use in the New Kingdom and persisted down to the latest times (Fig. 48). In Ptolemaic times it became a frequent custom to discard the single envelope of cartonnage, and to use a number of separate units. One piece covered

143

the head and shoulders, another placed upon the chest was adorned with representations of amulets and jewellery, and a foot-piece on which the details of the feet or sandals were painted was placed over the legs and feet. For a fine example of this method of using cartonnage we may refer to the frontispiece, which represents a mummy of the Ptolemaic period found in Nubia.[1]

It may be mentioned that waste-papers, i.e. fragments of old papyrus documents, were largely used in making cartonnage. From the mummy-cartonnage of Ptolemaic and later periods a large series of valuable classical texts has been recovered.

THE CANOPIC JARS.

The name of " Canopic Jars " has long been applied to the four jars in which the viscera were placed after they had been removed from the body and separately embalmed. They are generally of very fine workmanship and usually bear inscriptions. They have been found in tombs of the Old Kingdom,[2] which proves that their use goes back to very ancient times, and although no organic remains have survived from the early dynasties, it is evident that evisceration was practised in the process of mummification even at that early period, a fact which is confirmed by early mummies having embalming incisions (see p. 76).

In the Middle Kingdom their use was still continued, as many instances show. In the XIth Dynasty Tomb of Senebtisi at Lisht, for instance, four canopic jars were found with their contents still in them.

---

[1] Examples of the various methods of using cartonnage are too numerous to necessitate any references being given. Specimens can be seen in all museums and in the reports of numerous excavations in the course of which they have been found.

[2] Reisner : *The Dated Canopic Jars in the Gizeh Museum* in the *Ägyptische Zeitschrift*, t. xxxvii (1899), pp. 61 ff.

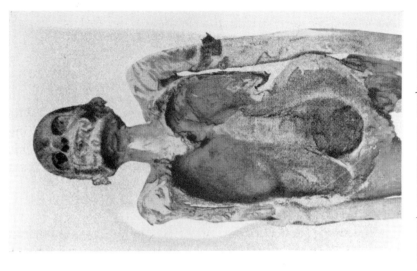

FIG. 62.—MUMMY OF A PRIEST OF AMEN (XXIst DYNASTY) AFFLICTED WITH POTT'S DISEASE.

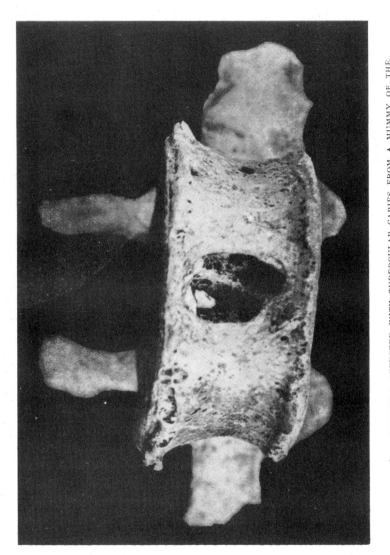

FIG. 63.—VERTEBRA AFFECTED WITH TUBERCULAR CARIES FROM A MUMMY OF THE MIDDLE KINGDOM

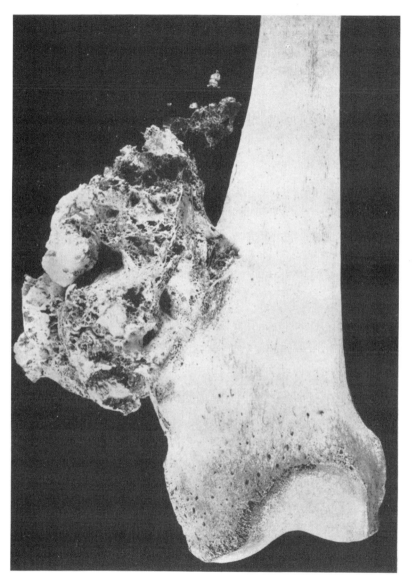

FIG. 64.—OSTEO-SARCOMA OF THE THIGH-BONE. (Vth DYNASTY)

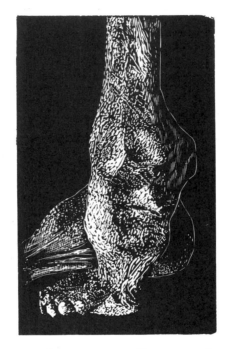

FIG. 65.—TALIPES, OR "CLUB-FOOT,"
OF THE PHARAOH SIPTAH

CANOPIC JARS

The stoppers or lids of these jars were fashioned in the shape of human heads until the end of the XVIIIth Dynasty, after which they bore the heads of the four children of Horus—one with a human head, one hawk-headed, one jackal-headed and the fourth ape-headed. These jars, when sealed, were placed in a chest or coffer, which may be seen drawn on a sledge in the pictures of the funeral procession [1] and of which many examples have been found.[2] (Fig. 49).

The sets of jars never exceed four in number and are never less than four, each jar being identified with one of the four children of Horus. The viscera were wrapped in four separate packages : (1) containing the liver which was identified with Imsety, (2) containing the stomach with Duamutef, (3) containing the lungs with Hapy, and (4) containing the intestines with Qebeh-snewef (Figs. 50 54).

It is commonly stated in such text-books as refer to embalming that *all* the viscera were removed from the body and put into canopic jars, Imsety receiving the stomach and large intestines, Hapy receiving the small intestines, Duamutef the heart and lungs, and Qebeh-snewef the liver and gall bladder. This attribution, which has been repeated again and again, is copied from a statement made in 1837 by Pettigrew [3] in the case of a single mummy where carelessness on the part of the embalmer led to the wrong attribution of the viscera in this instance. As the result of the examination of a large series of mummies the correct attribution stated above was arrived at.[4]

---

[1] See above, p. 40.

[2] For examples see Mace and Winlock : *The Tomb of Senebtisi*, Pl. VIII (XIth Dynasty) ; Brunton : *Lahun*, Pl. XIV (XIIth Dynasty) ; Quibell : *Tomb of Yuaa and Thuiu*, Pls. XIV and XV (XVIIIth Dynasty).

[3] *Transactions of Society of Antiquaries*, April 1838 (" The Jersey Mummy ").

[4] Elliot Smith : " Contribution to the Study of Mummification in Egypt," in the *Memoires Inst. Egypt*, t. v, fasc. i, 1906.

EGYPTIAN MUMMIES

It will be observed that no account is here taken of the heart and kidneys. Diodorus Siculus expressly mentions that the heart and kidneys were not excised with the other viscera (see above, p. 63). An examination of very many mummies proves that the heart is always left *in situ* and attached to the great vessels (see Fig. 38), except in a few cases where through careless manipulation the heart was wholly or partly severed. In such cases it was replaced in the body and never wrapped up with the other viscera.

With reference to the kidneys the case is not so clear. At the time of the XXIst Dynasty the general custom of putting the excised viscera into canopic jars was given up,[1] and it became the practice to wrap up each viscus along with a wax model of its appropriate guardian deity (Figs. 50–54), and restore it to the body (Fig. 50). Occasionally the kidneys were found (in the same series of mummies examined as mentioned above) in parcels of viscera associated with one or other of the deities ; more often they were found in parcels apart from those which contained the wax images of the children of Horus, and in many cases the kidneys were not recognisable in any of the parcels. The fact that the kidneys were thus not definitely associated with any one of the four funerary genii, when considered in conjunction with the statement of Diodorus, might perhaps be regarded as evidence in favour of the view that it was the intention of the embalmers to leave the kidneys, like the heart, in position in the body, and that some special significance attached to these two organs, which made it undesirable that they should be removed from the body along with the

---

[1] For the decline in the use of canopic jars see *Journ. Eg. Arch.*, t. v, p. 273, note 2. Dummy vases were sometimes put into the tomb to perpetuate the ancient practice long after their real function was lost. Some canopic jars of the XXIst Dynasty belonging to the family of the priest-kings are known, but they were very sparingly used at this period.

other viscera. The fact that the kidney was sometimes actually removed is presumably evidence merely of carelessness on the part of the operator, such as happened occasionally in the case of the heart also.[1]

For a general archæological account of the canopic jars and of the texts inscribed thereon the reader is once more referred to Gardiner's *Tomb of Amenemhēt* (p. 113).

AMULETS.

The use of amulets in connexion with burials in Egypt was very widespread and survived from pre-dynastic right down to Christian times.

These amulets, which are of very various kinds, were all endowed with potent magical virtues and gave protection to the deceased from all the dangers of the future life. The very bandages in which the body was wrapped, as we have seen from the *Ritual of Embalming*, all had magical names, and each one was an amulet, the gift of a god or goddess. The mummy is commonly called " this god." The hieroglyphic sign for " god " is itself a roll of cloth,[2] and it appears amongst the pictures of supplies provided for the dead on many coffins of the Middle Kingdom. In the *Tanis Sign Papyrus* the sign *ntr* (god) is defined as *iwf kris*, " it is buried " or " embalmed," i.e. ceremonially bandaged and assimilated to Osiris.[3]

In the New Kingdom it became customary to bury with each mummy a papyrus roll inscribed with a number of magic spells. This collection of spells is the well-known *Book of the Dead*. The entire roll containing these spells

---

[1] For a full discussion of the treatment of the viscera see Elliot Smith : *Journal of the Manchester Oriental Society*, vol. i (1911), pp. 45 ff.

[2] Griffith : *Hieroglyphs*, Pl. III, fig. 26, and p. 144.

[3] Griffith : *Two Hieroglyphic Papyri from Tanis*, p. 16.

was in itself looked upon as an amulet of great power, and small models of rolled-up papyri made of faience and other materials are often found in great numbers in tombs.[1] Other books besides the *Book of the Dead* written on papyrus were from the XXIst Dynasty onwards buried with mummies. The roll was generally placed between the legs and enclosed within the bandages, a good instance being the XXIst Dynasty priestess with the *Book of Him Who is in the Netherworld* unrolled some years ago at Cairo.[2] In later times still we find extracts from the *Pyramid Texts*, the old funerary book of the Pyramid Age,[3] the *Book of Breathings*,[4] and shorter works of the kind published by Birch and by Speleers.[5]

Amongst the numerous spells in the *Book of the Dead* are many which relate specifically to amulets, and in the rubrics directions are given as to the use of them. The following may be mentioned :—

Spells 19 and 20 [6] (R. 57–59, N. 194).—This text which occurs only in late papyri deals with the Crown of Justification, which is a floral wreath or garland to be placed upon the head of the mummy. Floral garlands are not uncommon

---

[1] E.g. Tomb of Tuthmosis IV. See Carter-Newberry: *Tomb of Thoutmosis IV (Cairo Cat. Gen.)*, pp. 114 ff. and Pl. XXV.

[2] Elliot Smith : *Annales du Service*, t. vii, Pls. V and IX.

[3] Renouf : *Life-Work*, t. ii, pp. 385–399.

[4] British Museum, No. 9995. *Papyrus of Kerasher* (ed. Budge).

[5] Birch : *Proc. Soc. Bibl. Archæology*, 1885. Speleers : *Rec. de Travaux*, t. 39, pp. 25 ff. The two *Rhind Papyri* previously mentioned are funerary spells of the same kind, as are also the papyri published by Maspero : *Quelques Papyrus du Louvre*, pp. 58–72.

[6] We use the word " spell " in preference for the usual term " chapter." The abbreviations R and N respectively refer to the pages of Renouf : *The Egyptian Book of the Dead ; Translation and Commentary* (continued and completed by Naville), 1893–1904, and to Naville : *Das ägyptische Todtenbuch*, Berlin 1886, *Einleitung*, where the Egyptian titles of the spells are given in full. The text and variants, not cited here, are in tomes i and ii of the same work.

AMULETS

in Egyptian tombs, and several fine specimens were found in the Tomb of Tutankhamen. The mummies of Aahmes I and of Amenophis I were decked with floral garlands.[1] According to Gardiner[2] these garlands were placed on mummies in memory of the wreaths given to Osiris on his triumphant exit from the judgment-hall of Heliopolis.

Spells 26–29 *b* (R. 66–73, N. 195).—All have reference to the heart. They are spells for preventing the removal of the heart from the body, or for ensuring that the heart shall be restored to the deceased. As the heart was never (except accidentally) removed from the body during the embalming process, these spells have more meaning in them than was formerly supposed.[3]

These spells were often written on gems.[4]

Spells 30 *a and b* (R. 74–75, N. 195).—Also relating to the heart, are very frequent both in papyri and also engraved upon large scarabs known as heart-scarabs.

Innumerable mummies have been found with heart-scarabs upon them.[5]

Spell 151 *A, ter* (R. 313, N. 202), is called the *Spell for the Mysterious Head,* the vignette being the head of a mummy, also doubtless an amulet.

Spell 155 (R. 325, N. 202).—"The *dad* of gold to be placed upon the neck of the glorious one." Amulets of this kind are common in all materials, especially blue faience, and are placed in almost any position on the mummy or laid among the wrappings. The *dad* is often found in the

---

[1] Maspero : *Les Momies Royales,* Pl. IV.
[2] *Tomb of Amenemhēt,* p. 111 and footnote 3. Gardiner suggests that the " Wreath of Justification " may be the ultimate origin of the " Crown of Righteousness " (2 Tim. iv, 8).   [3] See p. 146.
[4] Renouf, *op. cit.* p. 74, note.
[5] For a full account of the heart-scarab and its text, together with translation and notes, see Gardiner, *op. cit.* p. 112, and for a partially unwrapped mummy with the scarab *in situ,* see *Annales du Service,* t. vii, Pl. V, fig 2.

canonical position (Fig. 55). Sometimes the *dad* is tied to the arm (Fig. 58).

It is the emblem of Osiris and is a frequent ornamental device in funerary shrines, where it is usually associated with the girdle-tie.[1]

Spell 156 (R. 326, N. 202).—The girdle-tie of red jasper. This amulet is a symbol of Isis. The rubric directs that it shall be placed upon the neck.[1]

Spell 157 (R. 326, N. 202).—The vulture of gold. This amulet is also to be placed upon the neck. This spell is not found earlier than the Saite period.

Spell 158 (R. 327, N. 202).—The collar of gold. This also is directed to be placed upon the neck.

Spell 159 (R. 328, N. 202).—The column of green felspar. The vignettes show this to be a model of a papyrus column. The rubric directs that the spell shall be written on the amulet, which is to be placed upon the neck.[2] In Fig. 56 this amulet is seen tied to the arm of the mummy.

Spell 162 (R. 330–32).—The hypocephalus. This is a late spell and does not occur in early copies of the *Book of the Dead*. The title is " spell for causing a flame to arise under the head of the deceased." [3] A long rubric directs that the spell shall be recited over the image of a cow in gold, and placed on the neck of the deceased, or painted on a new papyrus and placed under the head, and it is in this latter form that we know the hypocephali in late mummies.[4]

---

[1] Gardiner, *op. cit.* p. 112.
[2] The next spell, No. 160, is entitled " Giving the Column of Green Felspar."
[3] So Naville *in* Renouf : *op. cit.* p. 330.
[4] The text will be found in Lepsius : *Todtenbuch,* Pl. LXXI = Budge : *Book of the Dead*, text, t. iii, p. 22.

For pictures of hypocephali see Daressy : *Textes et Dessins magiques,* Pl. XIII, and Budge : *Meux Collection*, Pl. VI.

AMULETS

Spell 165 (R. 338–9).—This is a late text and is the last spell in the Turin *Todtenbuch*. It prescribes a series of magical words to be spoken over a figure painted " in blue with liquid gum." The drawing is to be that of a figure with " raised arm." [1] with " two plumes on its head, its legs apart, its torso a scarab-beetle."

The rubric adds, further, that the spell is to be recited " over a figure, the middle part of which is that of a man ; his arms are hanging down. The head of a ram is his right shoulder and another on his left shoulder. Thou wilt paint on one bandage the two figures of the god with the raised arm, and put it across the chest of the deceased, so that the two painted figures may be on his breast." [2]

There does not appear to be any mummy recorded upon which a bandage so drawn upon has been found.

Spell 166.[3]—Spell for the pillow. The pillow or head-rest is frequently found under the heads of mummies of all periods.

Spell 171.[4]—Spell for wrapping up the deceased in a pure garment.

This spell has hitherto been found in one papyrus only [5] and is not really part of the *Book of the Dead*. From its mention of the gods Amen and Mont it evidently is of Theban origin and may, as Naville suggests, belong to the *Ritual of Amen*.

Mummies of all periods are found bedecked with countless

---

[1] I.e. the god Min.

[2] In Renouf (Naville), *op. cit.* Pl. LVIII, the vignettes of these two figures are reproduced from the Turin papyrus. The first mentioned is the god Min in his usual attitude, but with a scarab for his body.

[3] Naville *in* Renouf, *op. cit.* p. 340. Birch : *Aegyptische Zeitschrift*, 1868, p. 82.

[4] *Op. cit.* p. 347.

[5] Mariette : *Pap. de Boulaq*, t. iii, Pl. VII = Budge : *Book of the Dead*, text, t. iii, p. 53.

amulets, including those mentioned above and many others.[1] (See Figs. 50–54.)

A late hieratic papyrus in the Louvre [2] containing the *Book of Breathings*, and translated many years ago by de Horrack,[3] has on the verso a demotic rubric giving certain directions as to bandaging.

" The *Book of Breathings* which must be placed upon the side of the god (i.e. the deceased) on the outside of the innermost wrappings. It must be placed in his hand upon his heart, and it must then be wrapped in a cloth of fine linen, so that it is placed between his hand and his breast ; then the rest of the bandaging must be proceeded with.

" The *Book of Breathings* is that which Isis made for Osiris." [4]

Figures of gods and other devices are often drawn in ink upon the wrappings of mummies. Thus the mummy of Ramesses III had a bandlet round the head inscribed with figures of sacred vultures and uræi, and on removing the outer shroud a large drawing of a ram-headed bird with outstretched wings was disclosed.[5] In the XXIst Dynasty a large figure of Osiris was often traced upon one of the shrouds.[6]

Finally, reference may be made to embalming-plates. These have frequently been referred to above in describing

---

[1] A detailed list of the amulets found upon a single Ptolemaic mummy will be found in Daressy : *Annales du Service*, t. iv, pp. 80–83. See also the very full list of the amulets found on an XIth Dynasty mummy in Mace and Winlock : *Tomb of Senebtisi*, pp. 121 ff.

[2] Deveria : *Cat. Manuscrits Egypt.*, iv, 4 (3284), p. 132. Revillout quotes it as No. 2891 in *Aegyptische Zeitschrift*, 17 (1879), p. 92.

[3] An English version of de Horrack's translation is in *Records of the Past* (second series), t. iv, pp. 119 ff.

[4] The demotic text is reproduced by Revillout : *Aeg. Zeit.*, 17 (1879), Pl. VI, No. 23.

[5] Maspero : *Les Momies Royales*, Pl. XVII.

[6] *Annales du Service*, t. vii, Pl. VI, fig. 1.

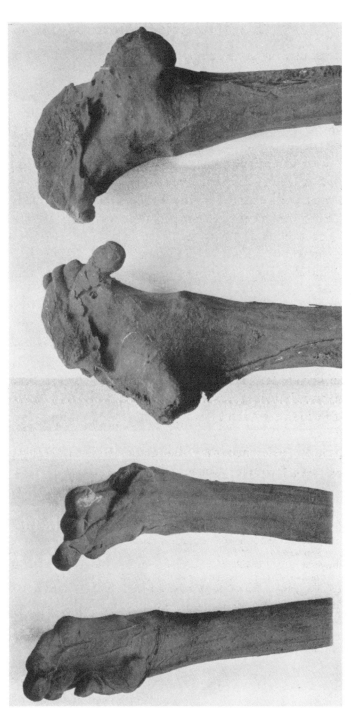

FIGS. 66 AND 67.—HANDS OF A MUMMY OF A COPTIC CHRISTIAN AFFLICTED WITH LEPROSY (6th CENTURY A.D., NUBIA), AND FEET OF THE SAME MUMMY

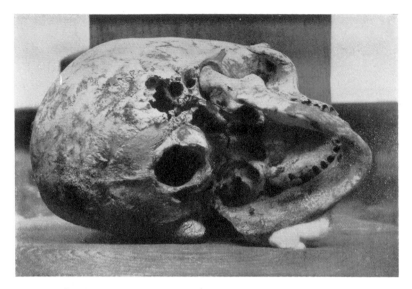

FIG. 68.—PREDYNASTIC SKULL, SHOWING THE DESTRUCTION OF THE
MASTOID PROCESS BY DISEASE

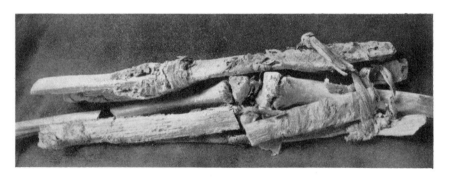

FIG. 69.—BROKEN FORE-ARM OF A Vth DYNASTY MUMMY SET IN SPLINTS

individual mummies, and are usually of wax, gold or other metals. These plates were laid over the incision in the left flank. The earliest forms are simple leaf-like plates, uninscribed. Towards the XXIst Dynasty a rectangular type was used, usually inscribed with the sacred eye in order to confer protection to the body (see Figs. 57 and 58). The magnificent specimen found on the mummy of Queen Henttaui (*supra* p. 117) had not only the symbolic eye, but figures of the four children of Horus who had especial care of the viscera. The function of these embalming-plates was clearly intended to be that of magic amulets affording protection to the viscera, and their position over the embalming-wound indicates that they acted as guardians over the orifice through which the organs were extracted, and in the XXIst Dynasty restored to the body.

CHAPTER X

MUMMIFICATION IN RELATION TO MEDICINE AND PATHOLOGY

WE have already called attention to the fact that the history of mummification touches that of medicine at many points. During the many centuries of the practice of embalming in Egypt men were constantly being reminded of the similarity of the human structure to that of animals used for food, so that even if there is little evidence of the acquisition of exact anatomical knowledge, it is altogether inconceivable that the long familiarity with the organs of the human body and their homologies with those of other mammals could have failed to influence the growth of knowledge of the human frame. And in fact, we know from such records as the Edwin Smith papyrus and the Ebers papyrus that the Egyptians had knowledge of certain parts of the body and their functions which for many centuries the Greeks lacked. But even more important than the positive gain in knowledge which the practice of mummification brought about was the influence it exerted in other ways on the progress of anatomy and the science of medicine in general. By familiarising the people of Egypt during the course of thirty centuries with the idea of cutting the dead human body, it was responsible for over-coming the popular prejudice against systematic dissection, which prevented Greek physicians from acquiring a know-ledge of practical anatomy in their own country. But public opinion in Egypt was such that no insuperable

MEDICINE AND PATHOLOGY

difficulty stood in their way : so that they were able to dissect in Alexandria from the third century B.C. onwards.

The practice of mummification affected the history of medicine in other ways. By familiarising the embalmers with the properties of many resins, balsams, and other mineral and vegetable substances used in the practice of their art, it gave them knowledge of their antiseptic properties, which afterwards led to their being included in the pharmacopœia. But great as was the direct influence of the various kinds of knowledge and experience on the history of medicine, the art of mummification probably exercised an even greater influence in shaping the theory of disease and methods of cure. For the whole body of principles of magical procedure and treatment of disease in early times was intimately bound up with the beliefs that prompted the practice of mummification. The arts of both the embalmer and the physician were concerned with devising means of protecting the individual from dangers to his existence, and the magical procedures in each case aimed at the giving of life, or rather at the renewal of the vital substance which was supposed to be deficient both in cases of illness and in what we call death.

With these serious aspects of the bearing of the practice of mummification on the history of medicine we have no intention of dealing in this book. But in this chapter a brief sketch will be given of the actual signs of disease revealed in Egyptian mummies, and in the bodies of the earlier peoples of the period prior to the invention of mummification. The number of diseased conditions which it is possible to identify in mummified bodies is strictly limited. Apart from the diseases which leave some definite record in the bones, it is possible only in rare cases to establish any kind of pathological process with certainty.

In mummies of different periods numerous cases of

calculi have been found; stone in the bladder has been found even as early as pre-dynastic times, and stones in the kidney occur in bodies of the IInd Dynasty. What is surprising about such cases, however, is their extreme rarity. Amongst the records of something like 30,000 bodies of ancient Egyptians and Nubians of which we have accurate records, only two cases of vesical calculus occur: one in a pre-dynastic body, the other one, curiously enough, inserted into the nostril of a priest of Amen of the XXIst Dynasty. Three cases of stone in the kidney have been recorded, and a single case of gall-stones (see Figs. 60 and 61). The first of these vesical calculi was submitted to very thorough examination by Professor Shattock, of the Royal College of Surgeons, London, but he was unable to find any trace of Bilharzia eggs,[1] although the most careful search was made. But some years later Sir Marc Armand Ruffer found Bilharzia eggs in a mummy of the XXIst Dynasty.[2]

Several cases of arterial disease have been found in the course of our investigations. One of these was examined in detail by Professor Shattock, whose report on the case has been published.[3] Others were described in the *Journal of Pathology and Bacteriology* for 1911 by Sir Marc Armand Ruffer.

During the course of the examination of the mummies of the priesthood of Amen of the XXIst Dynasty a case of Pott's Disease was found (Fig. 62) with severe spinal curvature and a large psoas abscess, to which reference has already been made and a description of which was published in Sudhoff's Journal in 1910.[4]

[1] *Trans. Pathological Soc. of London*, vol. lvi (1905), p. 275.
[2] *British Medical Journal*, January 1, 1910.   [3] *Lancet*, January 30, 1909.
[4] G. Elliot Smith and Marc Armand Ruffer in *Zur historischen Biologie der Krankheitserreger*, Heft 3, 1910.

MEDICINE AND PATHOLOGY

No true case of rickets or of syphilitic disease has been found in any ancient Egyptian remains. The much-debated problem of the occurrence of syphilis was discussed by one of us in *The Lancet* of August 22, 1908, where it was shown that there was no evidence whatever of any syphilitic injuries to the bones, nor anything even remotely resembling syphilitic injuries to the teeth. With reference to tuberculosis, in addition to the case of Pott's Disease mentioned above, a case of hip-disease was found in a body of the Vth Dynasty from the necropolis near the Pyramids, and a series of eight other cases of tubercular disease of the spine in Nubia.[1] (Fig. 63, from a mummy of the Middle Kingdom.)

A large osteo-sarcoma of the femur (Fig. 64) and two cases of sarcoma of the head of the humerus were found in the cemetery of the Gizeh Pyramids (Vth Dynasty), but no evidences of true cancer occur until comparatively recent (Byzantine) times, when cases of malignant disease involving the base of the skull and sacrum respectively suggest the presence of epithelioma of the naso-pharynx and rectum respectively. Only one case of cleft palate and one of talipes (club-foot) have come to light. The latter is the well-known case of the Pharaoh Siptah of the XIXth Dynasty. (See above p. 100 and Fig. 65.)

One of the most interesting cases brought to light is a perfect example of true gout. The subject of this disease was an elderly man; his long hair and beard were white, and the evidences afforded by his skeleton agreed with these indications of his age. He was a member of the local community of foreign Christians settled about the temple of Philæ. The feet, and especially the great toes, showed the

---

[1] *Bulletin of the Archæological Survey of Nubia*, No. 3, p. 31.

presence of the disease in the most striking manner. Large masses of white concretions were found on the metatarsal bones of the great toes, and the metatarso-phalangeal joints were the sites of these deposits, kept in place in the specimen by the tendons passing over them. The outer toes were affected to a lesser degree than the great toes, in which— on the left foot—one concretion measured 23 by 10 by 5 millimetres. Similar concretions were found encrusting ulcerated surfaces on the tarsal bones, and lower ends of the tibiæ and fibulæ ; the knee-joints were also affected, and upon the posterior surface of the patellæ, and in the patellar ligaments, were many chalky masses. The joints of the hands and of the arms showed the same chalky deposits, but they were not nearly so large as those in the feet and legs. The articulations of the carpus and meta-carpus showed the eroded patches, and the white masses ; and the humerus and radius of the right side were slightly affected. In addition to the signs of true gout, there were the typical inroads of the common osteo-arthritis ; the vertebræ, the shoulder-joints, and the left side of the jaw were the principal seats of its ravages.

The substance that composed the numerous white concretions was tested by Dr. W. A. Schmidt, and it was found to yield the typical reactions of uric acid. The specimen is now in the museum of the Royal College of Surgeons, London.

Both in Nubia and Egypt the ordinary form of dental caries is exceedingly rare in pre-dynastic and proto-dynastic people, and among the poorer classes it never became at all common until modern times. But as these people ate coarse food mixed with a considerable amount of sand, the teeth rapidly wore down, and as the result the pulp-cavities became opened up ; in the fertile soil of the exposed dental pulp, septic infection found a much readier place of attack than the hard resisting enamel and dentine of the tooth itself afforded ; hence it is common to find alveolar abscesses without dental caries, but some of the royal mummies suffered from both. Most of the dental disease of the archaic Egyptians and the poorer classes of the ancient Nubians in all periods is to be explained in this way.

But dental caries, although extremely rare before the Pyramid Age, became common as soon as people learned luxury. In the cemetery of the time of the Ancient Empire, excavated by the Hearst Expedition at the Gizeh Pyramids, more than five hundred skeletons of aristocrats of the time of the pyramid-builders were brought to light, and in these bodies it was found that tartar-formation, dental caries and alveolar abscesses were at least as common as they are in modern Europe to-day. And at every subsequent period of Egyptian history one finds the same thing—the wide prevalence of every form of dental disease among the wealthy people of luxurious diet, and the relative immunity from it among the poorer people who lived mainly on a coarse uncooked vegetable diet. There is in no case the slightest suggestion that any operative measures were adopted in order to cope with dental trouble, and in spite of frequent statements to the contrary, tooth-stopping was never practised in ancient Egypt.

The various pathological changes in bones and joints which are grouped collectively under the title of " rheumatoid arthritis " are so common in the bodies of all periods that it is true to say that " rheumatoid arthritis " is *par excellence the* bone disease of the ancient Egyptian and Nubian.

It is a condition of the very greatest interest, for it dates back—and with increasing frequency—to the earliest period of time with which we have to deal ; it is therefore a disease of great antiquity and wonderful prevalence, for the pre-dynastic Nubian scarcely ever grew to adult life without experiencing some of its effects. It is also of interest for the reason that its manifestations are legion, and to its varied types nearly all those diseases, the effects of which may be found in bones, have at one time or another been ascribed. Not only is the disease remarkably common, but in its natural progress it often reached stages of very great severity. Its trivial manifestations in some cemeteries are practically universal in adults, and its grave ones are far from rare ; and the specimens that illustrate this disease in our series are a remarkable collection of distorted joints and mishappen bones.

In the mummy of a woman of the Byzantine period in Nubia a case of the adhesions of an old appendicitis was found. The thickened band of adhesion passed from the appendix and became attached to the opposite side of the pelvis.[1] In the same cemetery a case of pleural adhesions was also recorded. In this case the left lung was collapsed and shrunken, and was firmly bound to the chest wall by a series of old adhesions.[2]

Reference has already been made (p. 119) to the mummy of an aged priestess of Amen of the XXIst Dynasty. This woman had suffered from a pelvic abscess and had developed extensive bed-sores, which the embalmer had carefully hidden under neatly adjusted sheets of gazelle-skin leather (Fig. 37).[3]

It is a curious fact that in a country where one might have expected leprosy to be common, only one case has been found, and that of early Christian date (Figs. 66, 67).[4]

Mastoid disease was very common in Egypt and in Nubia. From the latter country a large series of skulls affected with

---

[1] *Arch. Survey of Nubia, Bulletin* No. 1, p. 32, Pl. XXIV.
[2] *Idem, Report on Human Remains*, p. 268.
[3] *Mém. Inst. Egypt.*, t. v, fasc. i, p. 25.
[4] *Arch. Survey of Nubia, Bulletin* No. 6, p. 29.

FIG. 70.——MUMMY OF AMENOPHIS III (XVIIIth
DYNASTY) AS DISCOVERED IN THE COFFIN
OF RAMESSES III

FIG 71.—HEAD OF A FEMALE MUMMY, SHOWING THE FLOWING HAIR

mastoid disease was found and studied, showing various developments. A typical instance is seen in Fig. 68. Various other forms of cranial ulceration have likewise been found.[1]

Ramesses V, as already mentioned, suffered from a skin disease, the distribution and appearance of which strongly suggest small-pox (Fig. 28) ; but the exact diagnosis cannot be established with certainty : but the Pharaoh was unhealthy in other respects (see above, p. 105).

Fractures of the bones, especially the forearm, were extremely common. Hence it is not surprising that splints for the treatment of such injuries have been found as early as the IVth Dynasty (Fig. 69).[2] Splints of the same curiously distinctive type are still in use in the Sudan and Abyssinia, as well as in Borneo (and elsewhere in the Malay Archipelago). After the mummy of the Pharaoh Siptah had been badly maltreated by grave-robbers, the priests who restored his broken mummy set his fractured arm with splints of the same kind,[3] and other examples were found in Nubia in an early Christian cemetery.

It is a curious fact that, although the Edwin Smith Papyrus [4] suggests considerable surgical knowledge in Egypt seventeen centuries before the Christian era, there is a complete absence of evidence, in all bodies hitherto examined, of surgical procedure apart from the use of splints.

The use of a skinned mouse, presumably for the treatment

---

[1] *Arch. Survey of Nubia : Report on the Human Remains*, pp. 284 ff.

[2] G. Elliot Smith : " The Earliest Splints," in the *British Medical Journal*, March 28, 1908.

[3] *The Royal Mummies*, p. 42, fig. 14.

[4] This interesting papyrus has not yet been published, but Professor Breasted has given three preliminary accounts of it : (1) *New York Historical Society's Bulletin*, April 1922, pp. 4–31 ; (2) *Recueil Champollion*, Paris 1922, pp. 385–429 ; (3) *Bulletin of the Society of Medical History of Chicago*, vol. iii, January 1923, pp. 58–78.

of serious illness in children, is a fact of exceptional interest, for in the alimentary canals of the bodies of several children in the pre-dynastic cemetery of Naga-ed-Dêr, remains of this small animal were found which suggests that it had been skinned and administered as a final medicine to children *in extremis*. The mouse has continued as a children's medicine down to the present day, and is a custom of wide geographical distribution. The survival in popular medicine at the present day of a remedy which was already being used at least sixty centuries ago is without parallel.[1]

The only reliable account of the pathological conditions found in the mummies and skeletons of the ancient Egyptians and Nubians is that given by Wood Jones in the Annual Report for 1907–8 of the Archæological Survey of Nubia, of which a special volume of 375 quarto pages deals with the human remains.

---

[1] G. Elliot Smith : *The Ancient Egyptians*, 2nd ed., p. 50, and see also W. R. Dawson : *The Mouse in Medicine*, to appear in vol. x of the *Journal of Egyptian Archæology*, Pt. ii (1924).

CHAPTER XI

CONCLUSION

IN the preceding chapters we have sketched the history of mummification in Egypt through a span of more than thirty centuries. Egyptian writings suggest that the practice of embalming must originally have been devised to render the body of the dead king incorruptible, so that he might continue his existence indefinitely as the god Osiris. Thus it was regarded as a divine art in the sense that it was essential for conferring the boon of immortality which transformed a mortal king into a god. But if it was indeed the exclusive privilege of kings at first, it was soon adopted by the aristocracy also—for the earliest mummies that have come down to us from antiquity are not those of members of the royal family.

In course of time the practice of mummification became more and more widely democratised, until at the beginning of the Christian era it had spread to the whole population; and perhaps this fact may have played some part in preparing the way for the adoption of the Christian doctrine that the attainment of immortality was not the privilege of kings and nobles but was open to all mankind.

But Egyptian art was not only widely diffused among the people of Egypt, but had also spread to other countries. In the course of their trafficking with neighbouring peoples, in Nubia and the Sudan, in the Mediterranean islands and coasts, in East Africa and the Erythræan coasts, Egyptians had introduced many of their customs and practices. No doubt on many occasions Egyptians died abroad and were buried in accordance with their own customs. But long settlement in some of these places led to the adoption by the local people of the Egyptian custom of mummification; and when in later times the population of these colonies imitated their teachers and exploited countries still further afield, a variety of modified forms of Egyptian embalming were handed on stage by stage to distant lands, until every continent in the whole world was practising some of the many varieties of Egyptian mummification in a more or less modified form.

People in Nubia and the Sudan have been practising every stage of the art known in Egypt itself; but elsewhere in Africa only certain phases of mummification were adopted —for the most part the varieties of technique distinctive of the New Empire or later. Father Delattre found in Carthage a series of tombs belonging to the seventh and sixth centuries b.c., containing not only unmistakable Egyptian mummies but also representations of Egyptian deities.[1] But we know that the practice spread further around northwest Africa until it reached the Atlantic coast, as far as the Canaries and Nigeria. But from Egypt the custom also spread up the Nile and along the Red Sea coast, across the Continent to the Niger and Congo and to Uganda, and eventually even as far as Southern Rhodesia and Madagascar. It spread to Asia and was adopted for a time in India and Ceylon, but has persisted more widely in Further India, in Indo-China, in the Malay Archipelago, in Australia, Melanesia and Polynesia and reached Peru, Central America

---

[1] *Les grands Sarcophages anthropoïdes du Musée Lavigerie à Carthage*, and *La Nécropole punique de Douïmes*, quoted by Louis Reutter : *L'Embaumement avant et après Jésus-Christ*, Paris 1912, pp. 76 *et seq.*

CONCLUSION

and Mexico, and became widely diffused in both Continents of America.

We do not propose to discuss in this book the spread of mummification or the unmistakable evidence it affords of the reality of the diffusion of early culture. Some of the voluminous evidence in substantiation of these statements has already been given elsewhere.[1] We have referred to the matter here only because the survival of Egyptian methods of embalming in these other places for twelve or more centuries since they were abandoned in Egypt itself opens the possibility of getting information concerning many points in the process which we cannot now discover in Egypt itself.

This applies especially to the difficult problem of identifying the materials used for embalming in Egypt. For instance, such a work as Joseph Lanzoni's *Tractatus de Balsamatione Cadaverum* (Geneva 1696) gives a great deal of information concerning the preservatives that were used in Europe in the seventeenth and earlier centuries. Many if not most of these were survivals from much earlier times in the Eastern Mediterranean.

The use of butter as packing material for the mouths of Egyptian mummies 1000 B.C. assumes special importance when we recall Roscoe's account of a similar practice among the modern Baganda of East Africa, and the ritual importance attached to it. Then again, the insertion of mud and onions into the bodies of Egyptian mummies of the same period (XXIst Dynasty) becomes something more than a mere fantastic curiosity, when we discover that the Kilba of Northern Nigeria still adopt this strange method with the

---

[1] For the bibliographical references see G. Elliot Smith, *The Migrations of Early Culture*, Manchester 1915.

definite idea of retarding decomposition.[1] But what are much more important are the suggestions we get from methods of preservation used in modern times elsewhere, concerning which Egyptian writings are dumb. From the study of Egyptian mummies it is impossible to discover what measures were taken to desiccate the corpse. We know that the viscera were removed and that a variety of preservative agents were employed (resins and salts) in preparing the mummy. We know also that the peculiar technique used in the XXIst Dynasty necessarily involved the draining of moisture from the tissues of the corpse. But we also know that in practically every place where ancient methods of preserving the bodies of the dead have survived into modern times, special methods are used (in addition to the application of preservative agents) for drying the body. In some localities the skin is punctured and the body massaged to get rid of superfluous moisture ; in others it is exposed to the sun ; in other places, again, hot sand is applied to the body ; but far more widespread than any of these methods is a process of smoking or drying the body over a fire. In his account on the condition of the late mummified bodies in the First Annual Report (1907–8) of the Archæological Survey of Nubia, Wood Jones called attention to the fact that considerable heat must have been applied to some of the bodies. The evidence provided by the methods still used in many places in Africa, Australia, Oceania, and America tends to confirm his inference. The use of fire in connexion with the ritual of embalming, not merely for drying the corpse, but also for burning incense, suggests that the practice of cremation may have arisen (possibly

---

[1] O. Temple : *Notes on the Tribes, Provinces, Emirates and States of the Northern Provinces of Nigeria,* Cape Town 1919. (We owe this reference to Mr T. F. McIlwraith.)

CONCLUSION

in Sumer) for the ritual purpose of translating the dead man to the sky just as the offering of the incense was believed to bear to the sky-world the animating influence of the divine substance.

Scores of details in the Egyptian methods of embalming, such as the treatment of the skin, nails, hair, and brain, the special attentions paid to the head, hands, and reproductive organs, the use of paint and amulets, of incense and libations, and the wrapping and coffining of the dead, become more intelligible when we study these procedures as they are practised at the present day.

Whole chapters would be needed if we were to attempt to discuss the practices associated with mummification in Egypt which have survived in other lands—the making of portrait statues, the use of funerary couches, the religious significance of animal standards, the sacred dances and the varied ceremonial. But enough has been said to illustrate the manifold links which the ritual of embalmment had forged throughout the world in ancient times.

In many countries where mummification must have been adopted in early times and soon abandoned, scores of practices genetically linked up with embalming in Egypt have survived. Instead of attempting to preserve the body, for example, in parts of China, jade, pearls, cowries or gold are inserted into the mouth of the corpse under the belief that these materials will magically preserve the body. This can have no other meaning than that the practice in question is merely a surrogate of embalming.

We do not propose to discuss the nature of the materials used for embalming in Ancient Egypt. The important memoir published by Reutter in 1912 [1] gives the most reliable

---

[1] *L'Embaumement (op. cit. supra).*

information concerning the identification of the salts, resins, balsams, aromatic woods, and bitumens used in Egypt and elsewhere in Northern Africa. Other information has been given by W. A. Schmidt and A. Lucas.[1] The meaning of the divergence of opinion between Schmidt and Lucas is explained in the discussion reported on page 148 of *The Cairo Scientific Journal*, and also in Reutter's criticism of Lucas's methods (*op. cit*). It can be confidently stated that at most periods common salt (mixed with certain natural impurities) was the essential preservative agent employed by the Egyptians for embalming. Crude natron was used for mixing with resins to form a paste, and it was also mixed with shed parts of the body (such as the epidermis). The woods of various aromatic trees, and especially junipers, were also used. The analyses made by Reutter of the resins, balsams and woods reveal the wide extent of the geographical area exploited by the Egyptians to obtain materials for mummification. If a series of mummies of all the different periods were examined with proper scientific thoroughness it would be possible to reconstruct the foreign relations of Egypt at each epoch from the resins, the woods and the asphalts and bitumens found upon the mummies.

The realisation of the possibilities in the scientific examination of mummies is being realised, but when the possibility of getting the necessary material is becoming more and more remote.

---

[1] W. A. Schmidt : " Chemical and Bio-Chemical Examination of Egyptian Mummies, including some Observations on the Chemistry of the Embalming Process of the Ancient Egyptians," *The Cairo Scientific Journal*, April 1908. p. 147. See also above, p. 72 footnote. A. Lucas : " A Preliminary Note on some Preservative Materials used by the Ancient Egyptians in connexion with Embalming," *ibid.*, p. 133.

APPENDICES

APPENDIX I

THE TOMB OF TUTANKHAMEN AND THE ROBBERIES AT THE ROYAL TOMBS

THE wonderful discoveries made by the late Earl of Carnarvon and Mr. Howard Carter in the Tomb of the Pharaoh Tutankhamen have naturally raised the greatest interest in Egyptian burial customs. The special interest in this tomb lies in the fact that it is intact, or nearly so, and in this respect is unique, for although on rare occasions the tombs of private individuals have been discovered inviolate, such a thing has never before happened in the case of a king's tomb. The great quantities of jewellery, gold and other precious articles deposited in the tombs have throughout the ages made them the object of the greatest cupidity, and very, very few have escaped the ravages of ancient plunderers.[1]

The mutilated and battered mummies of the Kings described in previous chapters show clearly enough that the robbers were no respecters of persons, and it happens that antiquity has handed down to us a number of documents (papyri and ostraca) dealing with the personnel and administration of the Theban necropolis which throw much light upon tomb-robbing, and it will perhaps be instructive to glance rapidly through some of them in the light of modern discoveries.

---

[1] See, for instance, the magnificent jewellery from a royal tomb of the Middle Kingdom, found by Petrie and described and illustrated in colour by Brunton : *Lahun I—The Treasure*, London 1920. Most of this jewellery is now in the Metropolitan Museum of Art, New York.

EGYPTIAN MUMMIES

It must be remembered that the eastern bank of the Nile at Thebes was the city of the living, in which the Pharaoh and his court resided and all the civil life of the capital was carried on. The western bank was the great necropolis, or city of the dead. Here the limestone cliffs are honeycombed with tombs, and in the plain below the great mortuary temples of the Pharaohs spread out in a long line, each succeeding King adding another in which his funerary cult should be celebrated and the canonical offerings and commemorations should be solemnised. The nobles and citizens combined the chapel and the tomb in one unit, but the Kings separated them, the temples standing apart from their sepulchres, which latter were excavated at some distance away in the wild and rocky gorge known as Biban-el-Moluk, or the Valley of the Tombs of the Kings. In this valley the tombs of nearly all the sovereigns of the XVIIIth, XIXth and XXth Dynasties have been found. Some were known and standing open in Greek times, as the graffiti on the walls show. Others have been hidden by drifting sand or by falls from the limestone cliffs above them, and have been rediscovered in modern times : all of them save one [1] were without occupants, the plunderers having stripped them in bygone ages.

When we behold the enormous mass of valuable and precious objects found in the small and modest tomb of Tutankhamen, who was a relatively obscure King with a short reign, our imagination will fail us if we try to picture the magnificence and extent of the burial equipment which must have filled the enormous tombs of such Kings as Sety I and Ramesses II, who had long and prosperous

---

[1] One *King's* tomb, that is. Several tombs of princes or minor personages have been found with their original occupants still in them—e.g. those of Yuaa and Thuiu, and of Prince Maherprē.

reigns (the latter over sixty years). The Tomb of Sety I is excavated over 300 feet into the mountain, and consists of about fifteen corridors and chambers, some of them of enormous extent; the Tomb of Ramesses II has twenty chambers, and many of the others have chambers equally numerous and extensive. The size and extent of these tombs make it easy to understand that a very large population of workmen must have been required to excavate, decorate, and care for them. The burials of Kings required armies of masons, sculptors, painters, scribes, and artizans of every description, together with their overseers, foremen, and administrative officials. These workmen, moreover, had to be housed, clothed and fed, which again implies builders, carpenters, butchers, bakers, weavers, and water carriers (these were most important, for a constant supply of water must have been carried up from the Nile for the needs of the thirsty workers in the torrid heat of the necropolis). In addition to all these, the finished tombs each had guardians and priests attached to its service, and, further, the necropolis had a special police force of its own.

Now, it is concerning this great population of workers who lived and worked in the service of the dead that the documents above referred to relate. Nearly every museum has texts of this nature, but the greatest collection is at Turin, and belongs mostly to the reign of Ramesses III and his successors—some two centuries later than Tutankhamen. From these fragmentary documents a mass of information can be gathered as to the wages paid to these workers, and innumerable details of disputes, arrests, illnesses, holidays, bonuses,[1] legal proceedings and the private

---

[1] We learn from Liverpool Ostracon, No. M.13625, that extra rations were given on certain feast days.

life of these people. We know that the Egyptians used no coinage until Greek times, and all wages were paid in kind ; each man having an allotted ration of corn, oil, vegetables, and clothes, which was paid from the royal treasuries monthly. No doubt many of the men were improvident and failed to make their rations last out until the next pay-day, but we cannot escape the conviction that the rations were very inadequate and that the numerous scribes and officials who acted as distributors were self-seeking and dishonest and appropriated much to themselves. The result was easy to see : discontentment and disorder were very prevalent, and a reckless and lawless spirit had free play among the workmen. One of them, a certain Pinebi, was a thorough scoundrel, and a papyrus [1] has come down to us which is an indictment of many counts wherein he is accused of theft, bribery, rape, drunkenness, unlawful conversion, tomb-robbing, and other misdeeds. There is a similar papyrus in the Turin Museum.[2] In another case [3] a workman complains that some of his fellows entered his house in his absence and stole bread, cakes and other articles of food ; they also drank his beer and overturned and wasted his oil. Numerous instances of theft and pilferage are likewise recorded, and where such crimes or disputes called for legal settlement, they were generally referred for arbitration to the oracle of the deified King Amenophis I, who became the local and special god of the quarter of the necropolis in which the workers lived. Thus the god identifies from a number of suspects the guilty party who had stolen some clothes.[4] In another case the oracle was

---

[1] Papyrus Salt, Brit. Mus., No. 10055.

[2] Pleyte-Rossi : *Papyrus de Turin*, Pls. LI–LX, but fragments are arranged in the wrong order. [3] Brit. Mus. Ostracon, No. 5637

[4] Gardiner Ostracon, No. 4, translated by its owner in *Proc. Soc. Bibl Arch.* February 1917, p. 43.

appealed to in order to settle the disputed ownership of a tomb which the plaintiff alleged to have been granted to his forefathers by King Haremhab.[1] Somewhat similar disputes as to the division of property were likewise dealt with.[2] Many of these cases were doubtless settled by human assessors, the parties drawing up their cases in writing.[3]

We have journals and day-books of the scribes and clerks of the works which record the days upon which the gangers were at work and those upon which they were idle.[4] We do not know whether this idleness was enforced or voluntary, but the " off-days," almost as numerous as the working days, and often for long periods consecutively, may have been due to various causes. In the first place, we know that some were holidays, which were spent by the men, " eating and drinking with their wives and children." [5] Other days were reserved for the celebration of religious feasts. Shortage of rations again is the probable cause of some of the prolonged stoppages, such as the strikes described below, and also non-arrival of supplies during periods of stress, when internal rebellion or external warfare happened to be in progress. We know that at about this period many strange happenings took place in Egypt, and we find a reference to " the year of the hyænas, when men hungered," [6] doubtless referring to a Libyan invasion, or again, " the year in which the revolt of the high-priest of Amen took place." [7] In addition to these records of the

---

[1] Berlin Papyrus, No. 10496, and Brit. Mus. Ostracon, No. 5624, translated by Erman : *Sitzb. d. Kön. Pr. Akad.*, 1910.

[2] Brit. Mus. Ostracon, No. 5625 ; Cairo Ostracon, No. 25242.

[3] E.g. the bargain for an ass, Berlin Ostracon, No. P.1121, and many others.

[4] Papyrus Lieblein at Turin, partly published by Chabas and Lieblein : *Deux Papyrus hieratiques de Turin.*

[5] Cairo Ostracon, No. 25234.

[6] Brit. Mus. Papyrus, No. 10052, verso 4, 8.

[7] Brit. Mus. Papyrus, No. 10053, verso 6, 22 ff.

movements of the whole gang, we have lists of attendances by named individuals, the cause of absence from work, usually sickness, being stated.[1] So frequent, indeed, is sickness, that we must suppose the cause lay largely in insufficient food and unhealthy working conditions. The sequel to dishonest distribution of an already inadequate ration finally broke out in the twenty-ninth year of Ramesses III as a strike amongst the necropolis workers. One of the most human documents which antiquity has bequeathed to us is the official diary of a scribe which records these labour disturbances.[2]

The workmen, exasperated with their lot, left their work and crossed the boundary walls of the necropolis, in a temper which can be gathered from the words of the report, which said, " They swore great oaths," and met behind the chapel of Tuthmosis III. On the next days they went further afield and gathered around the gateway of the temple of Ramesses II. A few days later they sent a deputation to the responsible officials, their spokesmen saying : " We have come, urged by hunger, urged by thirst ; we have no linen, no oil, no fish, and no vegetables. Send and inform Pharaoh, our good Lord, on our behalf, and send to the vizier, our overlord, that he may obtain for us the means of life." This appeal succeeded, for the text continues : " Rations for the month were handed out to them." This, however, was only a palliative, for a few days later the workmen crossed the boundary walls again, and one of them in his excitement ran grave risk of punishment by uttering the oath, " By the Sovereign whose powers are mightier than death." [3] Fair words and promises had

---

[1] Brit. Mus. Ostracon, No. 5634.

[2] Pleyte-Rossi : *Papyrus de Turin*, Pls. XLII ff.

[3] This was an oath of great solemnity, not to be taken in vain. It occurs in several papyri and ostraca.

no effect, and the strikers called on the guilty officials by name. From time immemorial corruption existed amongst all the high officials of the State, and only a very active King, or a public outburst of serious magnitude, had the effect of temporarily checking it. We cannot but sympathise with the workers in this strike, whom we see, from a careful study of the whole text, to have had a very legitimate grievance. They did not strike, as modern workmen do, for shorter hours, or higher pay ; they merely clamoured for what was already due to them and not paid. The contest lasted a long time, for the report contains the happenings of day after day, the workers continually becoming bolder, and the guilty officials more and more in fear lest their victims should report them to Pharaoh. Another strike is recorded in the reign of Ramesses IX,[1] also on account of wages being withheld.

These underpaid and hardworked men were employed in making the gorgeous furniture and costly equipment of the Royal Tombs, and, whilst they felt the pinch of hunger, the Pharaoh loudly boasts of the huge endowments he makes to the temples to propitiate the gods in the interests of his own soul. The endowments made by Ramesses III to all the great temples of Egypt are stupendous, and are detailed at length in the longest and best preserved papyrus that antiquity has spared us.[2] It is scarcely to be wondered at that the valuables deposited in the Kings' tombs and in the storehouses attached thereto were a constant source of temptation to which the workmen continually succumbed. Under the successors of Ramesses III these thefts became such a public scandal that, in the reign of Ramesses IX,

---

[1] *Papyrus Lieblein* at Turin.
[2] *The Great Harris Papyrus*, Brit. Mus., No. 9999. The amount of corn paid over annually to the temples far exceeds the allowance for the whole of the necropolis workmen.

a commission was appointed by the Vizier to inspect the tombs and report on their condition.[1] The inspectors found a number of tombs violated, including the Royal Tomb of King Sebekemsawef of the XIIIth Dynasty, which had been entered by tunnelling from a neighbouring tomb. This latter tomb has been found in modern times, and the tunnel made by the thieves, and all the particulars of the ancient report have been verified.[2] A second papyrus [3] contains the confession of one of the thieves when brought to justice, and he describes how he and seven companions stripped the gold and jewellery from the mummies of the King and Queen, and divided the spoil. Yet another papyrus [4] deals with the violation of the tomb of a certain Queen Isis (wife of Ramesses III) by eight thieves, presumably the same eight, and with the damage done therein.

To return to the Abbott papyrus, after detailing the names of the tombs visited and their condition, the narrative proceeds to report the apprehension of certain suspects on a charge of robbing the Tomb of Queen Isis. Their arrest was due to the officious mayor to the town, whose duty did not extend to the necropolis, but who evidently wished to score over his rival, and thereby prove his negligence. The result of the trial was to vindicate the necropolis officials and inculpate the mayor, for the evidence was proved to be false and the suspects were set at liberty.

On the back of the Abbott papyrus are two long lists of prisoners, many of them high officials whose complicity had been bought, and a fourth papyrus [5] gives in great detail

---

[1] *Abbott Papyrus*, Brit. Mus., No. 10221.

[2] Newberry : *Theban Necropolis*, p. 14.

[3] Amherst Papyrus. Newberry : *Amherst Papyri*, Pls. IV–VII.

[4] Papyrus at Turin. Spiegelberg : *Zwei Beitrage*, p. 12.

[5] *Papyrus Mayer A.* at Liverpool Museum, published by Peet : *The Mayer Papyri A and B.*

the trial of these persons. There were two separate trials, one for robbery from the tombs of two Queens of the XIXth Dynasty, the other for thefts from certain buildings called " Corridor Houses," which were probably workshops or repositories of some sort, in which metals and other valuable objects for use in the tombs were stored. Some of the prisoners were found not guilty, but many of the thieves were convicted, and all kinds of witnesses were called to support the case for the Crown, which must have been very carefully prepared. In this papyrus not less than 180 names occur of prisoners and witnesses.[1]

We have much still to learn concerning these prosecutions, which cannot be accomplished until four important papyri in the British Museum, at present unpublished, are made available to scholars.[2] Enough, however, has been said to show that the strongest measures were taken by the Government to protect the sepulchres of the dead, but how unsuccessfully the sequel will show. It must not be supposed that tomb-breaking was only perpetrated at the period we have just discussed. There is abundant evidence that tombs of all periods were plundered, and evidence, moreover, that most of the plundering was done by contemporaries who knew their way about and exactly where to seek their object.[3] Many tombs were plundered more than once. Thus the tomb of Tuthmosis IV, which was discovered in recent times, was literally knee-deep in broken pottery and furniture, the work of the robbers who rifled the tomb for

---

[1] A papyrus at Vienna relates to this same series of events (this is the *Papyrus Ambras*, published by Brugsch : *Ägyptische Zeitschrift*, 1876, pp. 1 ff.) and *Mayer B.*, at Liverpool, is a fragment dealing with a robbery from the tomb of Ramesses VI.

[2] The recto only of one of them (*Pap. Harris A.*) has been published by Newberry in his *Amherst Papyri* (Pls. VIII–XIV).

[3] See the interesting case described by Mace in the *Bulletin of the Metropolitan Museum of New York*, December 1922, pp. 4–6.

the second time. The first robbers had broken in probably soon after the King's burial, and it was in disorder in the reign of Haremhab, who, we learn from a hieratic inscription on the wall, had the burial restored and damage made good in the eighth year of his reign. The royal mummies, which were discovered in two batches, one hidden in a deep pit-tomb at Deir-el-Bahari, the other in the tomb of Ameno-phis II, are most instructive by reason of the inscriptions written upon them. Owing to the continual violation of their tombs, which the Government of the day could not prevent, the high priests of Amen restored the damage and moved the mummies of the Kings from tomb to tomb, endeavouring to safeguard them. Thus the bodies of Sety I and Ramesses II, his son, were restored and re-bandaged by order of the Priest-King, Hrihor, [in the sixth year of his reign. Ten years later he moved the mummies of Ramesses I and II from their own tombs into that of Sety I for greater security; and this proving useless, the three mummies from that tomb were carried into the tomb of Queen Anhapu. A later Priest-King, Menkheperre, had them inspected, and found that they had again been rifled, and caused the bodies to be rebandaged and repaired. The tomb of Queen Anhapu having proved insecure from attack, the mummies of Sety I and Ramesses II were transferred to that of Amenophis I. Here, apparently, they remained until the XXIInd Dynasty, when they were transferred, together with all the other royal mummies whose hiding-places were known, to the *cache* at Deir-el-Bahari, where they remained unmolested until our own times. In 1872 the Arabs discovered the hiding-place, and sold many of the smaller antiquities buried with the mummies to European tourists. The fact that the Royal Tomb had been found by the natives became evident from objects belonging to the family of the Priest-Kings of the XXIst Dynasty which made their appearance on the market, but no one suspected what was actually hidden in the tomb. The authorities did not succeed in extracting the secret of the tomb from its holders until 1881, when by order of the late Sir G. Maspero the tomb was cleared and all the mummies taken to Cairo, where they can now be seen.[1]

Instead of a tomb containing merely some members of the family of the Priest-King Hrihor of the XXIst Dynasty a large cave was discovered literally packed with mummy cases, many bearing historic names. Thus came to light bodies of some of the most famous Pharaohs in Egypt's history. They included Seknenrē of the XVIIth Dynasty who made war on the Hyksos invaders, Aahmosis I, Amenophis I, Tuthmosis I, II and III, Sety I, Ramesses II and III, and others, besides many of their Queens, sons, daughters and other relatives. Added to these there were several XXIst Dynasty Priest-Kings with their Queens. How this hiding was accomplished in secrecy is difficult to understand, owing to the great number of coffins which had to be transported from a distance and lowered down the deep shaft, some of them so heavy that a dozen men could scarcely lift them.

The Kings found in this *cache* ranged from the XVIIth to the XXth Dynasties, but the series was incomplete and several Kings were absent. Maspero, therefore, formed the opinion that a second batch must be hidden elsewhere, as the first tomb was filled to its utmost capacity. Excavations were, therefore, vigorously carried on in the neighbourhood, but without success. A few years later Loret, who began

---

[1] The full narrative of this discovery is a veritable romance of science. The discovery is dealt with *in extenso* by Maspero : *Les Momies Royales de Deir-el-Bahari*, a bulky memoir of 276 quarto pages. A briefer account will be found in the *Guide du Visiteur au Musée du Caire*, 4th French ed., 1915, pp. 362–366.

a search in the Valley of the Kings itself, was rewarded by the discovery of the tomb of Amenophis II, and in it lay the King in his own sarcophagus, together with a number of other mummies which had been moved thither from their own tombs for safety. The second batch included, besides Amenophis II himself, Amenophis III, Tuthmosis IV, Meneptah, Siptah, Sety II, Ramesses IV, V and VI, together with several queens and princesses. Some of these mummies were taken to Cairo, but six (including Amenophis II) were left in the tomb. Shortly after the discovery the natives broke open the iron door which had been affixed to the entrance and rifled the King's body once more, and it is therefore much open to question if it is really wise to leave the Kings in their tombs as has been strongly advocated in the case of Tutankhamen.

All the mummies had been sadly maltreated by the ancient plunderers, who smashed the bodies in order to take the jewellery and ornaments from them. Some seem to have been the victims of wanton spite. Such was the mummy of Ramesses VI, which was literally hacked to pieces (Fig. 29), and the priests who restored the mummy could merely make up a bundle of odd limbs and fragments in the outward semblance of a mummy. Many of the royal mummies had lost their original coffins and were put into any which could be obtained, some very inferior specimens quite unworthy of their royal occupants.

The mummy of Tutankhamen has rested within the gilded shrines in his tomb unmolested, and is the sole Pharaoh hitherto found who has escaped the doom of his peers.[1]

---

[1] The coffins in which the royal mummies were found form a volume of the Cairo Museum Catalogue. Daressy : *Cercueils des Cachettes royales*, Cairo 1909. Another volume is devoted to a minute description of the mummies them-

THE ROYAL TOMBS

In Appendix II a list of the Kings from Seknenrē to Ramesses XI is given with reference to the mummies and tombs of all that are known. From this it will be observed that the tombs of all but four have been discovered. The sites of some have never been lost, and others have long been known ; only those rediscovered in modern times have been noted in the column headed " Remarks."

There is one other ancient papyrus which gains special significance from the Tutankhamen discovery. There is in the Turin museum the architect's plan of the Tomb of Ramesses IV,[1] with particulars as to its construction and dimensions written in hieratic writing. In the centre of the burial chamber is shown the sarcophagus, and this is surrounded by five rectangles, the meaning of which has hitherto not been understood. We now know from the Tomb of Tutankhamen that these rectangles are the shrines or tabernacles which were erected, one inside the other around the sarcophagus.

selves. Elliot Smith : *The Royal Mummies*, 1912: many of these mummies have been described in preceding chapters.

[1] This plan was exhaustively studied by Dr. A. H. Gardiner and Mr. Howard Carter, in the *Journal of Egyptian Archæology*, vol. iv, 1917. It has recently been reproduced in *The Times* and other newspapers.

APPENDIX II

LIST OF THE SOVEREIGNS FROM SEKNENRĒ OF THE XVIITH DYNASTY TO RAMESSES XI OF THE XXTH DYNASTY INDICATING THOSE WHOSE MUMMIES AND/OR TOMBS ARE KNOWN

For the tombs in *Biban-el-Molûk* (The Valley of the Tombs of the Kings) the official numeration is used. For a description of these tombs in numerical order, see Weigall: *Guide to the Antiquities of Upper Egypt*, second edition, London 1913 (but see below, footnote 3), and Lefebure: *Les Hypogées Royaux de Thèbes*, Paris 1886–1890.

Dynasty.	Name.	Where Mummy Found.	Situation of Tomb.	Remarks on the Tombs.
XVII	Seknenrē	Deir-el-Bahari	Not discovered	
XVIII	Aahmosis I	Deir-el-Bahari	Not discovered	
XVIII	Amenophis I	Deir-el-Bahari	N. of Drah Abou'l Negga	Discovered by the late Lord Carnarvon and Howard Carter, 1914.
XVIII	Tuthmosis I	Deir-el-Bahari	Biban-el-Molûk No. 38	Discovered by Loret, 1899.
XVIII	Tuthmosis II	Deir-el-Bahari	Biban-el-Molûk No. 42	Probably the tomb of this King, but not quite certain.
XVIII	Tuthmosis III	Deir-el-Bahari	Biban-el-Molûk No. 34	Discovered by Loret, 1899.
XVIII	Hatshepsowet	Not discovered	Biban-el-Molûk No. 20	Discovered by Theodore Davis, 1903.
XVIII	Amenophis II	Tomb of Amenophis II	Biban-el-Molûk No. 35	Discovered by Loret, 1898
XVIII	Tuthmosis IV	Tomb of Amenophis II	Biban-el-Molûk No. 43	Discovered by Loret, 1903
XVIII	Amenophis III	Tomb of Amenophis II	Biban-el-Molûk No. 22	Discovered by Napoleon's Expedition.
XVIII	Amenophis IV	Tomb of Queen Thiy	Tell-el-Amarna	Tomb of Queen Thiy discovered by Davis, 1907.
XVIII	Smenkerē	Not discovered	Not discovered	
XVIII	Tutankhamen	Own tomb	Biban-el-Molûk	Discovered by the late Lord Carnarvon and Howard Carter, 1922.
XVIII	Ay	Not discovered	Biban-el-Molûk No. 23	A previous tomb had been made at Tell-el-Amarna.
XIX	Haremhab	Not discovered [1]	Biban-el-Molûk No. 57	Discovered by Theodore Davis, 1908.
XIX	Ramesses I	Not discovered	Biban-el-Molûk No. 16	

XIX	Sety I	Deir-el-Bahari	Discovered by Belzoni, 1817.
XIX	Ramesses II	Deir-el-Bahari	
XIX	Meneptah	Tomb of Amenophis II	
XIX	Amenmesses	Not discovered	
XIX	Siptah	Tomb of Amenophis II	Discovered by Davis.
XIX	Sety II	Tomb of Amenophis II	
XX	Setnakht	Not discovered [2]	
XX	Ramesses III	Deir-el-Bahari	Tomb No. 3 was begun by this King but abandoned.
XX	Ramesses IV	Tomb of Amenophis II	
XX	Ramesses V	Tomb of Amenophis II	
XX	Ramesses VI	Tomb of Amenophis II	Tomb No. 9 was built for Ramesses V and usurped by Ramesses VI.
XX	Ramesses VII[3]	Not discovered	
XX	Ramesses VIII	Not discovered	
XX	Ramesses IX	Not discovered	
XX	Ramesses X	Not discovered	
XX	Ramesses XI	Not discovered	

Biban-el-Molûk No. 17	
Biban-el-Molûk No. 7	
Biban-el-Molûk No. 8	
Biban-el-Molûk No. 10	
Biban-el-Molûk No. 47	
Biban-el-Molûk No. 15	
Biban-el-Molûk No. 14	
Biban-el-Molûk No. 11	
Biban-el-Molûk No. 2	
Biban-el-Molûk No. 9	
Biban-el-Molûk No. 9	
Not discovered	
Biban-el-Molûk No. 1	
Biban-el-Molûk No. 6	
Biban-el-Molûk No. 18	
Biban-el-Molûk No. 4	

NOTES

[1] Some bones were found in the Sarcophagus of Haremhab, but in Theodore Davis' publication of the tomb (*The Tombs of Harmhabi*, etc.) no description is given of them, and no other mention than the brief note in the preface. Presumably they belonged to the King, but there are no data to enable the question to be settled.

[2] The coffin of this King was found in the Tomb of Amenophis II, but the mummy in it was that of a woman.

[3] In the classification of the later Rameside Kings we have accepted the revised numeration of eleven against twelve arrived at by Maspero's elimination of Sekhaenrē-Ramesses-Siptah, which he proved to be identical with Siptah (*Annales du Service*, t. x, p. 138). For purposes of identification we give below the full names of our Nos. VII–XI.

Ramesses VII, User-rē Mery Amen Yet Amen.
Ramesses VIII, User-rē Yakhenamen.
Ramesses IX, Nefer-ka-rē.
Ramesses X, Kheper-ma-rē.
Ramesses XI, Men-ma-rē.

For these identifications we are indebted to notes kindly supplied by Professor Newberry.

This nomenclature does not agree with that used by Weigall (*op. cit. supra*), but the identification of the tombs may be made by their numbers.

INDEX

Abbott Papyrus, 178
Abd'al-Latif, 19
Abydos, Journey to, 38
Adhesions—
  Appendicitis, 160
  Pleural, 160
Akhenaten, 95
Alveolar Abscesses, 99, 158
Ambras Papyrus, 179
Amherst Papyri, 65, 178
Amulets, 147
Anthony, St., 70
Anubis the Embalmer, 43, 48, 50, 51, 52
Appendicitis, 160
Arts and Crafts, 29
Augustine, 70

Bandages, 141
Bell, Mr. H. I., 64, 65
Blackman, Dr. A. M., 31, 35, 47, 60
Book of Breathings, 148, 152
Book of the Dead, 39, 67, 137, 148
Book of Gates, 139
Brain, *see s.v.* Cranial Cavity
Browne, Sir Thomas, 5
Butter used in Mummies, 115, 165

Calculi, 156
Cancer, 157
Canopic Jars, 40, 55, 144
Capart, Professor J., 9
Carnarvon, Earl of, 171, 184
Carter, Mr. Howard, 171, 184
Cartonnage, 143
Castration, 100
Circumcision, 75, 80, 93, 131
Cleft Palate, 157
Coffin-decoration, Significance of, 138

Coffin-texts, 45, 134
Coffins—
  " Civil-dress," 138
  Earliest, 133
  Græco-Roman, 140
  Middle Kingdom, 135
  New Kingdom, 136
  Old Kingdom, 134
  " Rishi," 136
  Saite, 140
Cornelius Nepos, 19
Cranial Cavity and Brain, 61, 68, 75, 81, 82, 89, 90, 123, 124
Crowns, Royal, 93
Crum, Mr. W. E., 69

Dad-amulet, 149
Death-bed, 34
Death-masks, 26
Decomposition, 125
Dental Caries, 158
Diaphragm, 85, 125
Diodorus Siculus, 18, 62, 146
Dioscorides, 19
Drugs for embalming, 24, 155, 168

Edwin Smith Papyrus, 154, 161
Embalmers' Workshop—
  Discovery of, 21, 37
  Egyptian Names for, 35, 54
  Escourting to, 60
  Lustrations in, 36
Embalming-plates, 152
Embalming-wound, 61, 63, 66, 76, 79, 81, 82, 88, 92, 98, 103, 105, 108, 115, 118
Emilius Probus, 19
Epidermis, 88, 101, 124, 168
Eyes, artificial, 104, 113, 114

187

INDEX